Woman's Guide
to Joyful Living

A Personal Study
of Philippians

Rhonda H. Kelley

NEW HOPE
PUBLISHERS

Birmingham, Alabama

New Hope® Publishers
P. O. Box 12065
Birmingham, AL 35202-2065
www.newhopepubl.com

Library of Congress Cataloging-in-Publication Data
Kelley, Rhonda.
A woman's guide to joyful living : a personal study of Philippians / by Rhonda H. Kelley.
p. cm.
Includes bibliographical references.
ISBN 1-56309-436-3 (pbk.)
1. Bible. N.T. Philippians-Textbooks. 2. Joy-Biblical teaching-Textbooks. 3. Christian
women-Religious life. I. Title.
BS2705.55.K45 2004
227'.6'0071—dc22
2004000093

ISBN-10: 1-56309-436-3
ISBN-13: 978-1-56309-436-1

N034103 • 0307 • 1M3

Other books in the Woman's Guide series
By Rhonda Kelley

A Woman's Guide to Spiritual Wellness

A Woman's Guide to Personal Holiness

A Woman's Guide to True Contentment

A Woman's Guide to Servant Leadership

A Woman's Guide to Personal Discipline

Rhonda Harrington Kelley

Rhonda Harrington Kelley is the author of every book in the Woman's Guide series, which includes to date: A Woman's Guide to Spiritual Wellness, A Woman's Guide to Personal Holiness (a 2002 selection in Crossings Book Club), A Woman's Guide to True Contentment, A Woman's Guide to Servant Leadership, and A Woman's Guide to Personal Discipline. She lives in New Orleans, where her husband, Chuck, is president of New Orleans Baptist Theological Seminary.

Dr. Kelley is a prolific writer, having authored or contributed to dozens of works, including coediting and contributing to The New King James Woman's Study Bible. She is a sought-after speaker, traveling the globe to address audiences about ministry involvement. She serves on the adjunct faculty at the New Orleans Baptist Theological Seminary, where she is the coordinator of the Women's Ministry Program. Dr. Kelley is also a radio and television host of the program "A Word for Women," broadcast in New Orleans, Louisiana, since 1983, and has served as associate director of Innovative Evangelism since 1978. She has also served as coordinator of the women's ministry committee since 1991 at First Baptist Church in New Orleans, where she and her husband are members.

Dr. Kelley holds a doctorate in Special Education and Speech Pathology from the University of New Orleans, and holds both a bachelors and masters in Speech Pathology and Audiology from Baylor University, where she was voted Outstanding Senior Woman. She served as a speech and language pathologist or consultant for nearly 20 years in medical and educational facilities before turning her attention to full-time ministry work.

A Woman's Guide to Joyful Living

TABLE OF CONTENTS

PREFACE

Have you seen frowns on many faces? Have you noticed the lack of luster in the eyes of friends and neighbors? Does it seem people today have lost their sparkle? It appears that the pleasant smile and radiant countenance is gone. Maybe everyone is tired. Or perhaps they are discouraged and hopeless. Even Christians seem despondent and lifeless. It is time for Christians to rejoice! We need a "spiritual makeover." We must find true joy in our hearts that will be reflected in our lives.

I am grateful to come from a godly background. Not only do I have a strong family of faith, I have parents who are joyful. As an evangelist, my dad, Bob Harrington, preached "It's Fun Being Saved." His message was so positive and uplifting. My precious mother always has a smile on her face, and her radiant countenance makes her look much younger than her years. Both parents taught me to be joyful and to have a positive attitude. By example and instruction they instilled in me a sincere sense of joy. I am so grateful to them!

When I was a teenager, a church soloist told me that she always looked at my mother when she sang. She said my mother's smile of encouragement sparkled from the congregation. I think of that so often, and I consciously smile as a member of any audience. Recently, a young deacon in our church commented about my joy as he passed the offering plate. He said, "I bet you fall asleep smiling. I have never seen you without a smile on your face." His compliment thrilled me. But it also holds me accountable. Every time I see him, I make sure that I have a smile on my face. As Christians, we should be joyful because we have so much to rejoice about.

In reality, we can always rejoice since we are not the source of our joy. True joy comes from God, not from ourselves, others, or our circumstances. Joy that is based on feelings or situations will be fleeting. But joy from the Lord will be lasting and real. Those who are unsaved cannot experience true joy. They must settle for temporary thrills and momentary pleasures. We have been promised eternal joy as we live the Christian life and then spend eternity with God in heaven.

Also, we have so much to rejoice about. God loves us and He has blessed us abundantly. Even in our trials, we sense the powerful work of the Holy Spirit. He gives us life itself as well as health and energy. He provides for our basic needs of food, clothing, and shelter. He surrounds us with loved ones—family members and friends who care for us. He gives us meaningful work and even times of leisure. God is so good! We must rejoice.

Joy should be an attitude of gratefulness in your heart. Your joy will bring glory to God and will rub off on others. Your joy should be contagious! God needs His children to spread His joy, His gift of grace, throughout the world. Will you do that? Will you make a commitment to joy and then be a catalyst for joy with others?

I am grateful that you have bought this book and begun this study. You can join me and many other Christian women in this joyful journey! Be assured of my prayers for you. I pray my joy will float off these pages and encourage your hearts. Your joy will be a blessing to me, too. So keep smiling!

—*Rhonda Harrington Kelley*

INTRODUCTION

A Woman's Guide to Joyful Living is the sixth book in a Bible study series for Christian women. Each Bible study is divided into twelve lessons and is designed for individual or group study. For a list of books in the series see the front of this book.

As you begin this study, make a commitment to the Lord to learn from Him and complete the course. You should determine a time and a place for your daily Bible study, then discipline yourself to do it. You may want to read through the short Book of Philippians several times and in different Bible translations.

Determine which Bible translation will be your primary source for study. (This Bible study uses the New King James Version unless otherwise noted.) And decide whether your study will be personal or shared with a small group. (You will find suggestions for group instruction in the back of the book.) Personal systematic Bible study is enhanced when shared in a group.

You may want to gather some resources that will support your personal study. In addition to your own Bible, secure several other Bible translations, a Bible dictionary, a general dictionary, relevant commentaries, and a Bible concordance. Of course, you will need a pen with ink (mine always seems to run out) and a colored highlighter to mark significant passages.

Each lesson is designed to focus on one passage of Scripture. We will work systematically through the book of Philippians, though we will approach the passage from a topical perspective. It's an interactive study, so you should read the background material, study the selected Scripture, answer questions, and make personal application to your own life. This Bible study has been written to include all three levels of study—observation, interpretation, and application.

A Woman's Guide to Joyful Living has been written as a 12-week study. Each lesson can be completed in one week, and the total study should be finished in twelve weeks. It is not a very in-depth study, so it should take about 30 to 45 minutes to complete each lesson. Try not to hurry through the study, but let God's Word penetrate your heart and life. This study is designed to provide spiritual growth for Christian women of all levels of spiritual maturity. Therefore, you can simply follow the flow of the study or supplement its content with extra materials. Most importantly, you need to personalize the study. Fit it into your schedule and make application to your own life.

When you have completed this study, I pray you will be overflowing with joy. The joy of the Lord can permeate your life no matter what your circumstances. But don't keep your joy to yourself. Share it with others. Let your joy be contagious. Let your joy be a testimony of God's grace. Others can find true joy if you will discover it yourself and pass it on to others. Rejoice and then let your joy in the Lord be known!

Philippians 1:1–11

It is easier to say "Rejoice in the Lord" than to do it! Joy is often an over-flow of happiness. When someone experiences blessing or achieves something good, joy is a natural reaction. But when things aren't going well, it is not easy to rejoice. The Bible says that Christians are to "rejoice always" (1 Thessalonians 5:16). Joy is a Christian virtue to develop even when facing challenging circumstances. The apostle Paul always rejoiced, though he faced many trials. In this lesson, we will study what it means to rejoice in the Lord—who should rejoice, how to rejoice, and why rejoice. We will learn from the most joyful apostle how to rejoice regardless.

What is joy? What does the word "joy" mean to you? Take a few minutes to reflect upon your understanding of this term, then write your own definition here.

Webster's Dictionary says *joy* is "the emotion evoked by well-being, success, or good fortune or by the prospect of possessing what one desires." To me, joy is a positive internal state of being that reflects itself in words, actions, and feelings. Joy overflows from a believer who is truly happy in the Lord. "Rejoice" is the active process of seeking joy; it is the emotional expression of joy.

A number of Hebrew and Greek words are used in the Bible to convey the concept of joy. The biblical meaning is actually "the happy state that results from knowing and serving God" (Butler, 1991). The word "joy" is found more than 150 times in the Bible (Butler, 1991). Thus, it can be considered a major theme of Scripture, a primary teaching of the Lord. True joy is dependent on a personal relationship with Jesus Christ. As a result, non-believers will never experience true joy. They must settle for momentary thrills.

Joy is included as a fruit of the Spirit, a virtue of those who walk in faith.

Before we study further, **read Galatians 5:22–23. What is the fruit of the Spirit in addition to joy? List them here:** _____, _____, _____, _____, _____, _____, _____, _____, _____.

The fruit of the Spirit refers to the godly attributes of those who "walk in the Spirit" (Galatians 5:16). Every believer, not just the spiritually elite, is to grow in faith and become more Christlike. Joy should be characteristic of every Christian. Unfortunately, not every believer is experiencing joy in the Lord. **What is your joy quotient? How joyful are you? On the scale below, mark your level of joy from 1 to 10. Be honest as you assess your present state of happiness.**

1_____5_____10
I am very unhappy.   I am sometimes happy.   I am always happy.

While some people are naturally happy or positive and others are naturally sad or negative, God desires for His children to be truly happy at all times. Joy is a manifestation of the presence and work of the Holy Spirit in the life of a Christian. It is not a character trait or personality style. Joy is a virtue of godliness. It is a desired goal for growing believers.

The Book of Philippians is about true joy. While numerous other themes are included and several key doctrines are explained, Philippians is Paul's letter of joy. Each of his New Testament epistles is a treatise to Christians about godly living. He taught joy by word and expression. When facing tremendous trials, his joy shone through. **Read the four chapters of the Book of Philippians, circling the words "joy" or "rejoice." Reread this short book often as a reminder to be joyful.**

Paul developed true joy as he grew in the Lord and walked in faith. His joy was unconditional—not based on circumstances. His joy was obvious—he talked about it constantly. His joy was contagious—those around him caught his joy. A study of Philippians will teach you about joy and help you rejoice. In this lesson, you will examine who should rejoice, how to rejoice, and why rejoice. Begin now to experience His true joy!

Who Should Rejoice?

Each New Testament letter, like correspondence today, begins with a greeting. In the opening sentences, the recipient or recipients of the letter are identified. However, the New Testament letter also identifies the sender in the opening verses, as well as the salutation and a prayer. Modern letters typically conclude with the salutation and writer's name. Paul's letters follow the format of most Greco-Roman letters of his day, containing an opening, the body, and the closing (Schreiner, 1990). As you read various letters in the New Testament, you will note similarities in content and style.

Begin your study today by reading the focal passage—Philippians

1:1–11. Identify the key people in the letter of Philippians, the characters who will teach us about joy. See Philippians 1:1 to answer the questions below.

Who **is the letter from?**

_____

Who **is the letter to?**

_____

The first word of the first verse of this book identifies the author—Paul. While Paul is familiar to many Christians, especially students of the New Testament, it would be helpful to remember his background and credentials. **What do you know about Paul? Write a brief biography of the apostle Paul.**

Much is known about Paul because of his prolific letter writing and the impact his ministry had on Christianity. Later in this study, you will examine a passage that is Paul's autobiography (Philippians 3:4–6). But for now it is important to recall that Paul (whose Jewish name was Saul) was born in Tarsus, was raised in a Jewish home, and was taught the Jewish Scriptures and traditions (Acts 22:3; 26:4–8). He studied the Jewish law and became a Pharisee, a member of the group of legalistic Jewish leaders (Butler, 791). As a Pharisee, he opposed the Christians because they refused the teaching of salvation through the law. Paul became a zealous persecutor of Christians (see Acts 8:1–3; 9:1–2; 26:9–11). But Paul was later converted. The public persecutor of Christians became a powerful proclaimer of the gospel to Gentiles and Jews alike.

Read about Paul's conversion experience in Acts 9:1–12 and his testimony in Acts 22:1–16. In the space below, describe Paul before his conversion and then after his conversion.

Paul Before Conversion—

Paul After Conversion—

Scripture records the dramatic conversion of Saul of Tarsus, who became known worldwide as Paul the apostle. The same man who once breathed "threats and murder against the disciples of the Lord" later "preached the Christ in the synagogues, that He is the Son of God" (Acts 9:1, 20). A once-terrifying tyrant became a powerful witness and missionary because of the transforming work of God. As a faithful servant of God, Paul wrote thirteen books of the New Testament, went on four missionary journeys, led many unbelievers to Christ, and started many early churches. During his ministry, Paul himself was persecuted for his faith. He was imprisoned several times and died while imprisoned in Rome.

Much is known about Paul and some is known about Timothy, who was also mentioned. In Philippians 1:1 Paul said the letter was from him and Timothy. He described both of them as "bondservants of Jesus Christ" (Philippians 1:1). How interesting that Paul didn't identify himself as an "apostle" as he did in most letters (Romans 1:1; 1 Corinthians 1:1; 2 Corinthians 1:1; Galatians 1:1; Ephesians 1:1; Colossians 1:1; 1 Timothy 1:1; 2 Timothy 1:1; and Titus 1:1). Maybe he wanted this letter to the Christians in Philippi to be from a personal friend, not a person in authority. It is known that Timothy was with Paul. He apparently ministered to Paul during his imprisonment in Rome.

Read the following passages in order to describe Timothy. Record a specific description from each reference below.

Acts 16:1–5

1 Timothy 1:1–2

2 Timothy 1:1–2

Timothy was a young disciple and frequent traveling companion of Paul. Together they spread the gospel and started churches. Paul mentored young Timothy in the faith and Timothy assisted Paul in ministry. He probably served as Paul's secretary in writing Philippians.

Timothy's father was Greek and his mother Jewish (Acts 16:1–5). Born and raised in Lystra, he was taught the Scriptures by his mother Eunice and his grandmother Lois (2 Timothy 1:5, 3:15). Paul was instrumental in

Timothy's conversion and advised him to be circumcised according to Jewish customs since they would be ministering to many Jews. Timothy was often Paul's representative to churches (Acts 17:14–15, 18:5, 19:22, 20:4; Romans 16:21; 1 Corinthians 16:10; 2 Corinthians 1:19; 1 Thessalonians 3:2, 6). And both names are listed as authors in six of the Pauline epistles—2 Corinthians, Philippians, Colossians, 1 Thessalonians, 2 Thessalonians, and Philemon. The relationship between Paul and Timothy was obviously very close. And Timothy's life and ministry were obviously strengthened by Paul the apostle.

Paul identified himself as a Christian who had reasons to rejoice. He also recognized Timothy as well as other Christians who should rejoice in the Lord. **Read Philippians 1:1 and describe the recipients of this letter below.**

Saints:

_____

Bishops:

_____

Deacons:

_____

To whom is Paul writing this letter?

This letter's initial intended audience was the church in Philippi, believers who had become true friends of Paul. He greeted them specifically, then individually recognized some leaders of the church—bishops and deacons. The letter was then shared with other congregations and continues to be read and studied by Christians today.

One of the primary themes of Paul's life and this letter was joy. He deeply desired for his Christian friends to be joyful. In fact, he understood that God wants all of His children to be joyful in all circumstances. So who should rejoice? It is a simple answer—every Christian. But it is not an easy answer. The practice of joy becomes a lifelong Christian discipline. Now let's consider how to rejoice.

How to Rejoice

The Bible is the most reliable "how to" book. It not only challenges Christians to godly living, it also gives guidance in godliness. After an initial greeting from Paul and Timothy to the church in Philippi and churches through the ages, Paul gave instructions for joyful living. He extended grace and peace in the name of the Lord and then taught us how to rejoice.

Read Philippians 1:3–8. How did Paul rejoice? As you read each

verse, complete the words below which describe how Paul expressed his joy.

r_____ (verse 3)

r_____ (verse 4)

f_____ (verse 5)

c_____ (verse 6)

h_____ (verse 7)

l_____ (verse 8)

Paul was filled with joy as he wrote this letter to his brothers and sisters in the Lord. He <u>remembered</u> them fondly (verse 3). He always prayed for them, making specific <u>requests</u> (verse 4). He enjoyed <u>fellowship</u> with them (verse 5) and he had <u>confidence</u> that God was working in their lives (verse 6). Paul rejoiced because he had his Christian friends in his <u>heart</u> (verse 7). And he <u>longed</u> to be with them again (verse 8). Paul was a joyful follower of Christ.

Do you know someone who is always joyful? What does that person's joy do for you?

The joy of a Christian is a positive witness for the Lord. A joyful Christian models for others how to rejoice. And their joy is contagious—it rubs off on others.

I try very hard to always be positive and joyful during stressful or challenging times. And I am blessed by the sweet spirits and joyful attitudes of others. Recently my precious sister-in-love Dorothy Patterson gave me some gold earrings from China. They are Chinese characters for the word "joy." In fact, each earring has two disks that spell out joy twice—JOY-JOY. Dorothy said that I bring two times as much joy to her as any other person. That loving gesture reminded me that joy is a blessing to all.

Joy is available through a faith relationship with Jesus Christ. He gives us His joy as we walk with Him. And we can share His joy with others. Paul learned that joy was from the Lord. And he learned that he could rejoice in everything. He rejoiced as he remembered the blessings of God, as he fellowshipped with other Christians, and as he served the Lord faithfully. That is also how we should rejoice. As we conclude this lesson, let's consider why it is important to rejoice.

Why Rejoice?

Joy is a key to spiritual growth. It is an essential attitude of the Christian's life. It is an evidence of godly living. In Philippians 1:9–11, Paul expressed his joy in praying for his Christian friends. He taught us how to pray so that we, too, can rejoice. As we share our joy and our sorrows with the Lord, we grow closer to Him. As we share the joys and sorrows of our friends, we encourage them.

Read Philippians 1:9–11. How did Paul pray for his friends? In the space provided below, list how Paul prayed specifically. We can learn to rejoice as we learn to pray for ourselves and others.

In this passage, Paul taught Christians how to pray and why to rejoice. Prayer should always be personal and from the heart, but prayer requests for others should always include several elements. Paul began his prayer by asking the Lord to give his friends love—not just a little love, but "abounding love" (Philippians 1:9). Throughout the Bible the virtue of love is proclaimed to be the greatest of all virtues. Paul himself began his discussion about the fruit of the Holy Spirit with love (Galatians 5:22). In 1 Corinthians 13 he declared that love was the greatest gift of all (1 Corinthians 13:13). Later in the New Testament, the apostle Peter stated that love covers a multitude of sins (1 Peter 4:8). When a believer has love, she can have joy.

Paul continued his prayer, asking God to give them knowledge and discernment (Philippians 1:9). Spiritual maturity is important for every believer. Paul knew that the Christians in Philippi would outgrow their petty differences and doctrinal confusion if they would increase in wisdom and knowledge. As they learned the Word of God and how to apply it personally, they could rejoice. But knowledge alone was not enough. Paul also felt they needed discernment.

Why do you think Paul prayed for both knowledge and discernment for believers?

What is your understanding of each of these mental activities?

Knowledge is important in the Christian life. But facts are not enough. A believer must also be discerning. We must learn what is good and bad, what is right and wrong, what is better and best. Knowledge and discernment can be powerful tools for the Christian's work.

Read Hebrews 5:14 and paraphrase its meaning in your own words.

The Lord desires for all of His children to be wise and discerning. It is only through spiritual growth as we learn more about the Lord that we can "discern both good and evil" (Hebrews 5:14). Discernment has always been crucial, but in an age where the world's view is so different from God's view, it is even more imperative. Paul prayed that the Christians would mature in their knowledge and discernment. Christians today need knowledge and discernment to distinguish truth from error.

Another request in his prayer was for Christlike or godly behavior. He prayed specifically for excellence of character, sincerity, and sensitivity for every believer (Philippians 1:10). The personal character of each Christian should reflect the image of God. Paul knew the joy of living a Christlike life and he wanted his Christian friends to experience the same joy.

Paul closed his prayer in this passage with a request for a fruitful life. He prayed that believers be "filled with the fruits of righteousness which are by Jesus Christ, to the glory and praise of God" (Philippians 1:11). Every Christian's life is to bear fruit just as a tree bears fruit. Jesus Himself declared, "By this My Father is glorified, that you bear much fruit; so you will be My disciples" (John 15:8).

The joy in Paul's life was a result of his spiritual growth. His abounding love, discerning choices, Christlike character, and fruitful life were reasons to rejoice. He wanted all Christians to rejoice in the Lord. We can rejoice like Paul if we understand who should rejoice, how to rejoice, and why rejoice!

 **LESSON TWO**  **REJOICE IN THE GOSPEL**

Philippians 1:12–18

Though the apostle Paul faced many challenges in his life and ministry, he always rejoiced. He rejoiced in the Lord at all times and in many ways. In the last lesson, we began this study of Philippians and sought to understand *who* should rejoice, *how* to rejoice, and *why* rejoice. The Bible clearly says that all people are to rejoice exceedingly and bring glory to God. What joy overflows from the life of a believer who focuses on the blessings of the Lord!

This lesson will consider the role of the gospel in the believer's life. Paul rejoiced not in his own efforts but in the Lord's work of salvation in his life. Because of his dynamic faith, Paul could rejoice in the gospel. Can you rejoice in the gospel? Before you answer that question, let us consider the meaning of the word "gospel."

Write a one-sentence definition of *gospel*.

Why is the gospel a reason for rejoicing?

Gospel is the English word used to translate the Greek word for "good news." It is much more than an exciting report from a friend, or long awaited results. Christians understand the gospel to be "the message and story of God's saving activity through the life, ministry, death, and resurrection of God's unique Son Jesus" (Butler, 567). So the gospel is the basis of our salvation—a message to rejoice about and share with others.

What good news from a family member or a friend have you heard about recently?

How did you respond when you heard that news?

The gospel of Jesus Christ is the best news any person will ever hear. It is cause for great rejoicing.

The Bible introduces the concept of good news in the Old Testament. The Hebrew word *bisar* was often used to express good news from the battlefield. When the Israelites won the battle against their foe, the military leaders sent good news of their victory (2 Samuel 4:10). Because of their faith in God, they proclaimed the good news of God's triumph over their enemies (Butler, 568). In addition, the Old Testament used the term *gospel* or *good news* in a personal sense. When God delivered His children from personal distress or danger, they proclaimed it "good news" (Psalm 40:9). Deliverance and salvation from God was the gospel to the Hebrew people.

The New Testament has a strong focus on the gospel. In His birth and life, the Messiah Jesus Christ brought the gospel. The gospel is actually the message preached by Jesus about faith in Him and the story of Jesus after His death and resurrection (Mark 1:14; Galatians 1:11–12). Another use of the word *gospel* is to describe the first four books of the New Testament, written by four disciples (Matthew, Mark, Luke, and John), which record the life and ministry of Jesus. Whether the promise of Jesus to provide redemption or the report by others of His sacrificial death to forgive our sins, the gospel is cause to rejoice. Now let's learn why it is essential to accept the gospel, defend the gospel, and preach the gospel.

ACCEPT THE GOSPEL

Jesus Himself explained the gospel as He began His ministry here on earth. Mark 1:14–15 says, "Jesus came to Galilee, preaching the gospel of the kingdom of God, and saying, 'The time is fulfilled, and the kingdom of God is at hand. Repent, and believe in the gospel.'" Each believer must personally accept this gospel message by professing faith in Jesus Christ. It is not enough to hear the gospel. Every individual must accept the gospel. Belief in Jesus and acceptance by faith releases the work of the gospel in the life of a person.

Paul experienced a dramatic conversion. Though he rejected the gospel and ridiculed Christians as a zealous Pharisee, he finally accepted Jesus

Christ by faith. **Recall the account of Paul's conversion in Acts 9:1–19. Why did the Lord offer Paul, a persecutor of Christians, salvation? Reread verses 15 and 16, then summarize your answer here.**

Salvation is offered to all people (Romans 1:16). The persecutor Paul was no exception. Saul, a devoutly religious Jewish leader who initially rejected the gospel was transformed by the saving power of the gospel. The persecutor became one of the boldest proclaimers of the gospel. **Now read Philippians 1:12–18 in several translations. What does Paul tell his Christian friends in Philippi about the gospel?**

Paul wanted other believers to know that the gospel not only changed his life but it continued to change the lives of others. Even his imprisonment could not stop the gospel. In fact, the gospel actually spread farther because of his imprisonment.

Pause for a few minutes to reflect on the gospel's impact on your own life. How are you different since your conversion?

I am grateful that the gospel has totally transformed my life. Not only has Christ saved me, but I live and work to spread the gospel. As a communicator, I am always seeking for the best words to express the gospel to others. As a teacher, I am working to challenge students to learn about the gospel so they can instruct others. As a writer, I am recording insights about the gospel to stimulate readers to greater faith. As a wife and woman, I am trying to live out the gospel in my life every day. I have experienced such joy as the gospel of Jesus Christ has completely changed me.

Paul told his friends that the gospel was impacting many people even though he was in prison. In Philippians 1:13, he identified those who had seen the gospel—"the whole palace guard and all the rest." Because of his imprisonment, Paul had an opportunity to share the gospel with people he may never have met otherwise. The soldiers and guards in the Roman prison were introduced to Jesus by a fettered follower. Paul's chains could not bind the gospel. The gospel spread freely not only in that prison but throughout the Roman Empire. Many converted soldiers became missionaries as the government sent them to serve in distant places. With joy and boldness, the gospel accepted by Paul was accepted by others.

On a recent mission trip to China, I met a precious Chinese Christian. The faith of the young woman was amazing. She explained that her father, a leader in the underground church, had recently been arrested. While she was sad to be separated from him, she rejoiced over his opportunity to share the gospel in prison. With great sincerity she said, "My Father can now proclaim the gospel without fear. He will win many people to Jesus who would never hear the gospel if he were free." The gospel of Jesus cannot be chained.

There is joy when a person hears the gospel and accepts Jesus as Savior. In the parable of the lost coin, Jesus told His followers that "there is joy in the presence of the angels of God over one sinner who repents" (Luke 15:10). The salvation of one soul is cause for great rejoicing. **Have you reason to rejoice? Has someone you know recently accepted the gospel of salvation?**
Who? _____

How has his/her life been changed?

Paul strongly proclaimed the power of the gospel to change his life and the lives of others—to spread despite his imprisonment. The gospel message was for all—Jews and Greek, slave and free, male and female (Galatians 3:28). Anyone who hears the gospel and believes it can receive Jesus Christ as Savior. Paul was also empowered to defend the gospel against its foes. Christians throughout history and especially today must stand up boldly to defend their faith—the gospel of Jesus Christ.

DEFEND THE GOSPEL

The truth must always be defended. There are always doubters who will question the truth. Believers must boldly defend the gospel they have accepted by faith. We must always "be ready to give a defense to everyone who asks you a reason for the hope that is in you" (1 Peter 3:15). However, many Christians are hesitant to share the gospel they have accepted. They are concerned about rejection or failure. They will miss out on the joy of the Lord if they do not boldly defend their faith.

Several times in his letters to the early churches, Paul challenged Christians to defend the gospel. Because there is a natural tendency to flee from trouble, Christians must learn to remain steadfast in the faith. Paul began his letter to the Christians in Rome with a testimony of his defense of the gospel even in challenging times. **Read Romans 1:16, then fill in the blanks in the Scripture below.**

"For I am not ashamed of the _____ of Christ, for it is the power of God to _____ for everyone who _____, for the Jew first and also for the Greek."

Because of his love for the Lord and concern for the salvation of others, Paul could not be ashamed of the gospel. He confidently defended its power to save all people. **Now read Paul's defense of the gospel in Galatians 2:1–10. Answer the questions below.**

How did Paul defend the gospel?

Why did Paul defend the gospel?

What happened to the gospel?

To the Philippians, Paul said that God had appointed him to be a defender of the gospel. He corrected those who spoke lies and rebuked those who had selfish ambition (Philippians 2:3). To the Galatians, Paul said false brethren must hear the truth of the gospel (Galatians 2:4–5). He spoke the truth boldly because of his passionate love for the Lord. Because of Paul's faithful proclamation, the gospel spread. If the gospel is not defended, the gospel will not continue on.

There may be times when you will be called on by God to defend the gospel, to stand up for what you believe. While it may be hard, the Lord will reward your obedience with great joy. **Can you recall a time when you obediently defended the gospel? When was it?**

What happened?

If you have defended the gospel, you should be stronger and you should be joyful. When the gospel is defended and truth is proclaimed, there is great celebration—abundant joy.

PREACH THE GOSPEL

Though Paul was a prisoner when he wrote this letter to the Philippians, he actually had more opportunity to share the good news. God had given him a task—preach the gospel in season and out of season (2 Timothy 4:2). Paul obeyed the Lord and preached the gospel faithfully. The message of salvation spread across the nations drawing many to faith in Jesus Christ. Paul experienced great joy as he preached even when he was a prisoner. He modeled for Christians today a commitment to spreading the gospel, the good news of Jesus Christ.

During his missionary journeys and while in prison, Paul had frequent opportunities to preach. Over and over again Paul shared his own dramatic conversion and challenged others to accept the gospel message by faith. In one of my husband's sermons, he said Paul kept singing the same song and same verse—"I was walking down the Damascus road when suddenly Jesus transformed my life, and what you see in me is only a mere reflection of what He wants to do in you." Paul preached the gospel consistently and powerfully.

In Philippians 1:15–18 Paul contrasts how the gospel should be preached with how it should not be preached. **Read those verses again then summarize the differences below.**

Preached for Self—

Preached for Others—

Sadly, the apostle knew that all people were not preaching the gospel unselfishly. Some preached Christ even "from envy and strife" (Philippians 1:15a). Their motives were totally selfish. They wanted attention and recognition, not genuine repentance. Some, according to Paul, were concerned for others. They preached the gospel "from goodwill" (Philippians 1:15b). He further differentiated them. The selfish preached selfishly, not sincerely, in order to hurt Paul and his witness (Philippians 1:16). Unfortunately, some contemporary preachers also have selfish motives. Paul rejoiced because some preached out of love for God and others (Philippians 1:17). Their messages supported the gospel preached by Paul. The faithful disciple rejoiced whenever the gospel was preached—in pretense or in truth—because Christ is proclaimed.

My husband and I recently attended a movie that was not a true presentation of the gospel, but God was the main character. In the movie, a man became God in the modern-day world. Initially he used his divine powers for selfish gain, but later he intervened to help others. Though fraught with biblical inconsistencies, Chuck and I both concluded that the viewers of the movie at least thought about God. We agreed with the apostle Paul in Philippians 1:18—"What then? Only that in every way, whether in pretense or in truth, Christ is preached; and in this I rejoice, yes, and will rejoice."

In another epistle, Paul wrote to young Timothy about preaching the gospel. He told him, "Do not be ashamed of the testimony of our Lord, nor of me His prisoner" (2 Timothy 1:8). Paul was bold in his witness, and he challenged Christians to imitate his evangelistic fervor.

Read 2 Timothy 1:8–12. Why did Paul say Timothy should not be ashamed of the gospel?

What does verse 12 teach about how we can boldly share our faith?

Paul clearly taught through his life and with his words that believers are to always unashamedly preach the gospel of Jesus Christ. Why? God has saved us and called us not because of who we are or what we have done but because He loves us. How can we boldly share our faith? Not in our own power, but in His power, knowing that "He is able" though we are not (Philippians 1:12).

Most Christians hesitate to share the gospel because of fear. Lack of confidence and dread of rejection paralyze the witness. **Have you ever experienced fear or panic when faced with defending the gospel? _____ How did you respond to your fear?**

What did you learn from your frightening experience?

Fear is a natural reaction for a Christian when faced with preaching the gospel. **Remember Paul's confession in 1 Corinthians 2:2? (Take time to read the entire passage in 1 Corinthians 2:1-5.)** If Paul could overcome his fear of witnessing through the power of the Holy Spirit, you can, too. All Christians can be empowered to defend the gospel. Just before his challenge for Timothy to defend his faith, Paul reminded him of God's power available to all believers. In 2 Timothy 1:7, Paul said: "God has not given us a spirit of fear, but of power and of love and of a sound mind." Confidence and strength come from God. And in His power, we can defend the gospel.

Paul's joy was visible. The gospel had transformed his life, and he had to share the gospel with others. Since he had accepted the gospel, Paul was committed to defending and preaching the gospel. Because he was a persistent proclaimer of the gospel, he could rejoice. Christians today can rejoice when we faithfully witness the changing power of Christ in salvation.

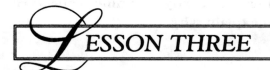

Philippians 1:19–26

The apostle Paul was transparent in expressing his deep feelings in every letter written to his Christian friends. He honestly shared his love for Jesus Christ. He clearly expressed his concerns about Christians who were not living their faith. And he openly admitted his personal struggles in the faith. That is why you and I can relate directly to Paul and his commitment to the Lord. He honestly shares his human emotions.

Paul began his letter to the Philippians with a focus on God— "He who has begun a good work in you will complete it" (Philippians 1:6). He continued with a discussion of the gospel— "I am appointed for the defense of the gospel" (Philippians 1:17). Then he admitted a spiritual battle within himself— "for to me, to live is Christ, and to die is gain" (Philippians 1:21). In each passage of Scripture, Paul's tone was exuberant. He rejoiced in the Lord, in the gospel, and in life. His desire was to encourage all Christians to rejoice even in the midst of struggles.

At this time you should slowly and carefully read Philippians 1:19–26. As you do, try to understand how Paul felt as he wrote to his Christian friends. What words or phrases in this Scripture passage describe the writer's feelings?

Paul was *eager* to be delivered from life's hardships, to be uplifted in prayer by other believers, and to be supported by the Holy Spirit (verse 19). He was also *hopeful* that he would never disappoint the Lord with shameful behavior and that God would always live and work through him (verse 20). Paul was also *confident* that God was with him and he would remain with his friends in spirit (verse 25). Because of his deep faith in God and his confidence in Him, Paul could rejoice. In fact, he wanted other Christians to experience the joy of faith "that your rejoicing...may be more abundant in Jesus Christ" (verse 26).

Do you share Paul's feelings? Honestly examine your own response to these questions and explain why.

Are you eagerly seeking God?

Are you hopeful about the future?

Are you confident in Him?

In another New Testament epistle, Paul expressed his desire to rejoice even in his sufferings. **Read Colossians 1:24–29. What did God teach Paul about the Christian life in that Scripture?**

Christ living in and through the believer's life is the only hope of glory (Colossians 1:27). That is why Paul worked for the Lord in such a mighty way (Colossians 1:28). God desires to work in and through you in a mighty way if you will eagerly seek Him, hopefully trust Him, and confidently follow Him. Then you will have a reason to rejoice and bring glory to God.

While it doesn't seem logical, Christians can rejoice as they struggle with who they are and how to live. Even when life is difficult, Christians can be strengthened by their personal faith in God, the prayers of others, and the presence of the Holy Spirit. When life gets tough, the believer may hope for the peace and joy of heaven. But in times of personal struggle, Christians should be confident in God's purpose for their lives here on earth. Ultimately, all Christians should seek to know and do God's best like Paul did. In this lesson, we will carefully examine what Paul learned about life, death, and God's best.

REJOICE IN LIFE

Have you ever been at a point in your life when you felt like Paul—"for to me, to live is Christ, and to die is gain"? Maybe you have been very sick and in pain and you truly wanted to die to get out of your misery. You may have been extremely depressed or despondent and wanted to die to be free of your loneliness. Those human feelings are natural responses to challenging situations. Paul was in prison because of his faith. He suffered physically and emotionally as he was tortured and kept in isolation. So to Paul, death seemed much more pleasant than life, especially since in death he would be present with the Lord. But Paul wanted God's will, not his own. Today we face the same dilemma—do we want to live with our human frailties or die and be in the presence of the Lord? We often wonder that for our loved ones.

Years ago my Granddaddy Harrington had a stroke. The strong, independent patriarch of our family was weakened physically and unable to care for himself. He spent the last months of his life in a nursing home. Though he was physically impaired, his spirit was not damaged. He was a blessing to all who visited him. His years of serving the Lord as a Methodist minister strengthened his faith and gave him a precious testimony. I remember one day when my sister commented that it would be better for him to die and be free of his suffering. The two of us then had that conversation about life and death. We concluded that God is the giver and taker of life, and that God must not be finished with Granddaddy yet. Even in his limitations, his life was good because his life was God's plan. In his weakness he was a blessing to us and many others.

Reread Philippians 1:19–26 attending to every comment that Paul makes about life. Prayerfully develop five statements based on Paul's beliefs that you can make about life, and complete the sentences below.

Life is

Life is

Life is

Life is

Life is

There are so many things to say about life because it is truly a gift from God. From the moment of conception, life is precious. Witnessing the birth of a baby is a miracle—God's miracle of life. Life is often filled with blessings and celebrations—graduations, marriages, and holidays with loved ones. But life is also tough; it is difficult. Often, challenging circumstances and events happen that make life hard. Life itself doesn't change for the believer at the time of conversion. But God promises to live life with His children, providing comfort, strength, and guidance. It is truly in the struggles of life that Christians draw closer to the Lord.

Paul determined that even in his difficult life, God would be glorified and magnified. He knew his ministry would draw more people to the Lord—that God still needed him to do His work on earth. So he decided to rejoice in life. In fact, he knew that everyone would joy in his life. He concluded this passage with confidence: "I know that I shall remain and continue with you all for your progress and joy of faith, that your rejoicing for me may be more abundant in Jesus Christ by my coming to you again" (Philippians 1:25–26).

Jesus Himself talked about life as He explained Himself to His disciples. Jesus said that He was the life and that He gives life to anyone who follows Him. His promise was not just to give some life, but to give abundant life—life beyond comprehension. **Read John 10:10 and paraphrase that verse.**

Because of Jesus, Christians can say, "Life is good!" While it isn't always easy, with God it can be good. Though it isn't always happy, with God it can be good. Though it isn't always perfect, with God it can be good. Paul concluded that life is good—"for to me, to live is Christ" (Philippians 1:21). In life, God can teach us more about Himself and work through us to accomplish His purpose. For the believer, death is always better, but God's will is best.

REJOICE IN DEATH

It is hard for unbelievers to understand how believers can rejoice in death. For the unsaved, death is the end—there is no more. For the saved, death is the beginning—eternal life begins. Therefore, Christians can rejoice at death, knowing that a believer is still alive, present with the Lord in heaven for all eternity. **Have you attended the funeral service of a Christian friend lately? How did you feel? Why could you rejoice?**

The loss of a loved one certainly brings sorrow. Their presence will be missed. But there is great comfort in knowing that a believer is no longer suffering, that the believer is in heaven. Jesus said, "he who hears My word and believes in Him who sent Me has everlasting life, and shall not come into judgment, but has passed from death into life" (John 5:24).

I have often attended the funerals of faithful Christians and have left the service in celebration, not sorrow. What a joy to celebrate the life of a servant of God! In fact, in one recent funeral the minister was so vivid in his description of heaven that I was ready to go! We believers have so much to look forward to in heaven. So we can say that death will be even better than life.

Read the following Scriptures about heaven. Then summarize what the Bible teaches about heaven.

Genesis 1:8—

Psalm 19:1—

Hebrews 4:14—

Paul knew and understood what the Bible teaches about heaven. That is why he wanted to choose death over life. Heaven is the vast expanse of space surrounding the earth (Genesis 1:8—"God called the firmament Heaven"). Heaven is the matchless celestial universe (Psalm 19:1—"The heavens declare the glory of God; and the firmament shows His handiwork"). And heaven is the longed-for dwelling place of God (Hebrews 4:14—"We have a great High Priest who has passed through the heavens, Jesus the Son of God"). For every believer, heaven is the promise of presence with the Lord for all eternity.

Paul longed for heaven not only to be present with the Lord, but to be free of pain and suffering (Revelation 21:1–7). All believers should anticipate heaven, but more importantly, we should live life in light of eternity. Life on earth is fleeting, while life after death is forever. The values and perspective of eternity should guide our lives in the present. **Read 2 Peter 3:10–13. How does God want you to live now in light of eternity?**

We are to live holy, godly lives to bring honor to Him and draw others to Him.

My precious in-laws spent their careers serving in the funeral business. They truly ministered to friends and families as they were mourning. In recent years as they have been aging, they have made arrangements for their deaths. They have purchased cemetery plots and installed a beautiful headstone. They have made funeral arrangements and even planned their services. In the meanwhile, they are living godly lives. They want their deaths to be a time of celebration, and they don't want their children burdened by details. What a special gift to their family. They are prepared to die while they are enjoying life.

Can you better understand Paul's struggle? Do you face the same dilemma? Life is good, death is better, but God's purpose is best. Our challenge as Christians is to persevere in faith until He comes, to grow in our knowledge of Him until we die, and to develop holy lives until we are transported to heaven. We can do that because God's purpose for our lives is best!

REJOICE IN GOD'S BEST

You may have had the same debate within yourself as Paul—do I want to live or die? When life gets very difficult, heaven becomes more desirable. But, like Paul, we must conclude that God's purpose is best. It was no accident that you were born—God created you. It will be no accident when you die—God will determine when. And your life in between, whether good or bad, is known by God. God has a plan and purpose for your life and death.

In this passage of Philippians, Paul could see the benefits of living and the benefits of dying. He realized that life meant "fruit from [his] labor" (Philippians 1:22) and was "more needful for you" (Philippians 1:24). But he longed for the promise of heaven and release from the sufferings on earth—"having a desire to depart and be with Christ, which is far better" (Philippians 1:23). Though he wrestled with that question, Paul concluded that God wanted him to stay a while longer, to encourage the saints and further build the kingdom (Philippians 1:25–26). Though he genuinely struggled with the decision, once it was made, he was confident. God's purpose for me is best!

Have you ever struggled with a major decision in your life like Paul? Maybe it wasn't between life and death, but between two jobs or two houses or two churches. What was your struggle?

What did you decide?

How did it turn out?

Just last year we faced a major decision with the Kelleys. As my father-in-law's health was declining, alternative living arrangements needed to be considered. The family approached this decision prayerfully. We read helpful books, visited numerous facilities, and discussed appropriate options. As the time came for a final decision, we made a list of pros and cons for each option to be considered. Then the decision became very clear. The choice was made and the move was scheduled. While the Kelleys did not choose their new life circumstances, they did seek God's guidance. After a year, we know that God's will was best. They are well cared for and very content in their new surroundings.

Christians must constantly make choices, big or small. It is our responsibility to always seek God's will and purpose, not our own. Several times in my life, I have struggled like Paul to choose what is best. When I have followed God's lead, it has always been best. Several years after our marriage, my husband and I realized that we would not be able to have children biologically. So we had to make a choice—do we adopt or not? There were advantages or blessings on both sides. We talked and prayed and thought and cried. But the whole time we prayed sincerely to do God's will. In time, each of us clearly understood that God's purpose for our marriage was not children but ministry. We both felt a peace about this very personal decision. In looking back, Chuck and I see God's hand on our lives and marriage. He has used us together in ministry in a greater way than possible with the responsibility of children. Children aren't bad—they are a blessing. For us, God's purpose was best. He chose for us ministry and love for other people's children. God has a purpose for your life, too! What a joy to face life and death knowing that God always has your best in mind.

LESSON FOUR REJOICE IN SUFFERING

Philippians 1:27–2:4

Suffering and adversity are part of every believer's life. The circumstances of life often bring hardship to even the most faithful follower of Christ. In fact, Jesus Christ Himself suffered during His life and as He faced death on the cross. His suffering is our model of how to respond to our own suffering. Jesus, who suffered in our place and for our sins, shows us a way to victory that transforms suffering into glory. We as Christians must be determined to rejoice even in our most extreme adversity.

Reflect on a time in your life when you suffered adversity. What were the circumstances?

How did you respond?

What did you learn through your suffering?

Job is the person in the Bible most well known for his suffering. He was a patriarch of the faith who loved God and lived a faithful life (Job 1:1). However, Job faced great adversity in his life. His faith was tested by Satan. Job lost his property, lost his children, and lost his health. In addition to all he lost, he also had to endure poor advice and inappropriate blame from his friends. Even his wife told him he should curse God and die (Job 2:9). Life for Job became unbearable by human standards (Job 17). Though he grew increasingly discouraged and defeated, Job was victorious and his faith was rewarded. If you haven't read the Book of Job recently, take time to read it.

In his weakness and pain, Job questioned God. Then God revealed His omnipotence to Job when He spoke out of a whirlwind (Job 38:1). With many rhetorical questions, God clearly reminded Job of His sovereign control (Job 38–39). Job responded to God without true confession and repentance. So God spoke to Job again about His power and judgment (Job 40–41). Job finally responded to the omnipotence of God and returned to his faith. **Read Job 42:1–17 and determine how a believer should respond to suffering. List below at least five lessons to be learned in suffering.**

1.

2.

3.

4.

5.

Job suffered greatly, but ultimately he learned a profound lesson. While God never explained why he had suffered, Job learned once again how to trust in God. When you face suffering, you must focus on your faith in God, not the circumstances of your suffering. Suffering should remind you of your own insufficiency and lead you to a greater faith in God. If you have faith in your adversity, then you can rejoice in suffering. You can rejoice for His sake, rejoice for your sake, and rejoice for their sake.

SUFFER FOR HIS SAKE

The suffering of a believer should be different from the suffering of an unbeliever. For the Christian, suffering is not in vain. When we suffer, we grow closer to the Lord and learn to suffer for His sake. In our suffering, we can testify to the love, strength, and care of the Lord. A Christian is not only to believe in the Lord but also suffer for His sake (Philippians 1:29).

While your suffering may seem very intense and unbearable to you, no one has suffered like Jesus. He suffered ridicule and scoffing during His ministry. But His greatest suffering was on the cross. He suffered for our sake and for God's sake. His death was a part of God's plan to give us salvation.

Remind yourself of Jesus' suffering on the cross as you read Matthew 27. List below several descriptions of how Jesus suffered to atone for our sins.

Each of the four Gospels records an account of the suffering of Jesus as He was convicted and crucified. (See Matthew 27, Mark 15, Luke 23, and John 18–19.) He experienced the greatest suffering of all time and He did it for you and me. He was persecuted by His enemies and betrayed by His disciple Judas. Matthew reports in chapter 27 that Jesus was bound (verse 1), accused (verse 12), convicted (verse 12), stripped (verse 28), crowned with thorns (verse 29), mocked (verse 29), spat upon (verse 30), and crucified (verse 31). Death by crucifixion was a cruel form of execution since it resulted in a long, slow death, mostly from asphyxiation. Not only was crucifixion extremely cruel, it was also very humiliating. The Jewish people hated this form of execution because of the Old Testament teaching—"he who is hanged [on a tree] is accursed of God" (Deuteronomy 21:22–23). Jesus Christ was accursed by God on our behalf. His shameful suffering atoned for our sins and provided us salvation. That is cause for rejoicing!

Christians can have joy because of the suffering Savior. If Jesus had not died on the cross to save us from our sin, we would experience much more suffering and pay the penalty for our sin. Because He was willing to suffer for us, we should be willing to suffer for Him. Christians often suffer for their faith. Sometimes religious persecution is only uncomfortable—rejection by others. Other times it is unbearable—physical beating or imprisonment. Religious persecution continues today and the persecution is often severe. Religious persecution is a reality in every part of the world.

Reflect back on times in your life when you have felt persecuted for your faith. Describe your experience here.

How did you feel?

How did you respond?

The first Christian martyr was Stephen, a courageous leader in the early church. He boldly proclaimed that Jesus was the Messiah and suffered at the hands of the Jews (Acts 7:54–60). As he was being stoned, Stephen glorified God: "But he, being full of the Holy Spirit, gazed into heaven and saw the glory of God, and Jesus standing at the right hand of God" (Acts 7:55). In his death, Stephen trusted in God. His sacrificial death for the cause of Christ was a powerful testimony to all, especially young Saul who later became a great Christian missionary. Saul, who was later named Paul, was first introduced in Scripture in Acts 7:58.

It is not uncommon today for Christians to suffer for the sake of the gospel. Recently three Southern Baptist missionaries were killed as they served the Lord in a hospital in Yemen. An angry gunman shot each of them at close range, then wounded several others. Though they had helped many Yemeni people in their years of ministry, one vindictive person took their lives unjustly. In their deaths, God was glorified. Many people came to know Christ because of their sacrificial commitments. The mission work in that closed country will continue and grow stronger because they were willing to suffer, even to die, for God's sake.

Jesus Christ suffered for the sake of His Father. Throughout history, Christians have suffered for the sake of their faith in God. You and I must be willing to suffer for God's sake, knowing that in suffering He will be glorified. Rejoice as you suffer for the Lord! And rejoice even as you suffer for your sake. God can teach you valuable life lessons through the tough times.

SUFFER FOR YOUR SAKE

Christians can experience joy in suffering if we understand His pain and learn from our pain. When we understand that Jesus suffered for our salvation, we can truly rejoice. But we must also learn to face our own suffering and grow through it. One of the major themes of the Book of James is rejoicing in adversity. He believed and taught that Christians are to "count it all joy when you fall into various trials, knowing that the testing of your faith produces patience" (James 1:2–3). Though it is a tough way to learn patience, aren't we grateful that maturity can result from our suffering?

Read James 1:2–8 to better understand why you should rejoice in your suffering. Summarize those verses in your own words in an effort to learn how to be joyful in suffering.

Personal suffering is often the consequence of our own sinfulness, sometimes caused by the sinfulness of others, and other times the result of circumstances. In each situation, suffering is painful. But the Christian can develop godly virtues like patience as she rejoices in her suffering. God can use the suffering to bring glory to Himself.

Many people in the Bible suffered as a result of sin or because of the circumstances of life. The story of Mary Magdalene relates her own suffering before her encounter with Jesus. Biblical accounts indicate that she was demon possessed (Mark 16:9; Luke 8:2). She suffered physically, mentally, and spiritually until Jesus cast out her demons. **Read the following Scripture references to understand how a person who was demon possessed might suffer.**

Matthew 8:28—

Matthew 9:32–33—

Matthew 12:22—

Mark 1:26—

Luke 9:39—

Demon possession was an extreme form of suffering. Its symptoms were severe and debilitating: violence (Matthew 8:28), speechlessness (Matthew 9:32–33), blindness (Matthew 12:22), convulsions (Mark 1:26), and foaming at the mouth (Luke 9:39). An individual who was demon possessed was tormented continuously. Mary Magdalene endured the suffering caused by her demons and was healed by a loving Savior. She then became one of His most faithful followers and loyal friends. Mary Magdalene was a witness of Jesus' crucifixion, burial, and resurrection. Her suffering was reason for rejoicing because it turned her to Jesus for salvation and healing.

Some suffering is punishment for sin. Whenever a Christian sins against God, consequences will be experienced. While consequences take on many forms, suffering may be the direct result of sin. Peter spoke about suffering imposed because of sin in 1 Peter 4:15–19. He warned that "the time has come for judgment to begin" (1 Peter 4:17) and urged, "let those who suffer according to the will of God commit their souls to Him in doing good" (1 Peter 4:19).

Take a few minutes to read 1 Peter 4:12-19 to better understand why suffering may be a result of sinfulness. What else does this Scripture teach about suffering? Explain the following phrases from this Scripture passage. Then rejoice in your own suffering.

"the fiery trial"—

"partake of Christ's sufferings"—

"reproached for the name of Christ"—

"suffer as a murderer"—

"suffer as a Christian"—

"suffer according to the will of God"—

Christians can be "glad with exceeding joy" because suffering is not in vain but is for the glory of God (1 Peter 4:13). In fact, Christians can be purified, strengthened, and edified through their suffering. Even the consequences of sin can help mold the believer into a holy life.

Jewelers have a process of gold purification. The precious metal is heated in order to remove impurities and create the purest form of gold. The purest gold is the most costly. What an enlightening analogy! When our lives become filled with sin, the Lord may have to purify with fire (suffering) so that we will become holy like Him. Christians may suffer to develop a pure heart.

Paul's instructions to the Christians in Philippi were clear—"let your conduct be worthy of the gospel of Christ...believe in Him...suffer for His sake" (Philippians 1:27, 29). That command should be followed today. If we are obedient to the Lord, we don't suffer in vain. Our suffering is for His sake and can bring glory to God our heavenly Father. Our suffering can also be a witness to others of our trust in Him.

In a recent conversation at a women's conference, I learned of the personal suffering of one woman. She had been a victim of sexual abuse herself and seen others in her family victimized as well. As she shared her story, her face radiated hope. God had saved her and restored her and was using her past pain to be a help to other hurting women. God is in the process of redeeming her pain for His glory, for her strength, and for help to others. She did not choose her suffering, but she chose to respond to it in faith. Her suffering has not been in vain—she is helping many others through her support group for hurting women. She is suffering for their sake.

SUFFER FOR THEIR SAKE

A believer who remains faithful in suffering can be a powerful testimony to others. Unsaved friends and family members can see how God strengthens His children in their times of suffering. Other believers are encouraged by spiritually mature Christians who persevere in their times of difficulty. God can use suffering to be a witness to other people of His care for His children.

First Peter 4:12–19 is a key New Testament passage on suffering. This Bible passage reminds Christians not to be confused or discouraged when they suffer, but to "rejoice to the extent that you partake of Christ's sufferings, that when His glory is revealed, you may also be glad with exceeding joy" (1 Peter 4:13). While it is true that the suffering of Christians can bring glory to God and strengthen their faith, the Bible also teaches that a Christian should move beyond her own suffering and "do good to others" (1 Peter 4:19). **Read this entire passage—1 Peter 4:12–19—then paraphrase verse 19 in your own words.**

God wants to redeem the suffering of the saints, and He can if we will glorify Him, strengthen our faith, and minister to others in our times of suffering.

There are three specific ways that Christians can suffer for the sake of others. In our suffering and as a result of our suffering, we can express *concern*, *comfort*, and *care* to them. God often uses our particular kind of suffering to prepare us to minister to individuals with the same problem. Because God strengthened me and deepened my faith when my dad, who was a minister, left the Lord and divorced my mother, I am able to understand the heartbreak of others who suffer the pain of divorce and encourage them from my own experience. There is a depth of concern for others when we have walked the same path.

Let's take a few minutes to think about the concern, comfort, and care we can extend to those who are suffering. While there are only subtle differences in the meaning of these words, **try to determine comparisons and contrasts in these words as you better learn how to reach out to others. Write a brief description of each word below.**

Concern—

Comfort—

Care—

Now think of another person who has faced a similar challenge as you. Who is she?

What is the struggle?

How can you minister to her?

I believe that *concern* is the emotion we feel when we recognize that another person is hurting. We can then show sympathy. A phone call to a sick friend, a card to a person who has lost a loved one, or a visit to a new neighbor indicates that you recognize a need and are concerned. But a Christian who has experienced a similar hardship cannot and should not stop there. Your concern should stimulate you to comfort them.

Comfort is a deeper emotion, expressed by one who has had the same feelings, thoughts, and experience. In relationship to others, you move beyond recognition or concern to personal understanding and empathy. A woman who has lost a child to miscarriage can comfort another woman in her loss because of a shared experience. A woman who has been diagnosed and treated for breast cancer can better support another cancer patient, and a woman who has herself been abused can encourage another battered woman. God uses our own suffering to comfort others. While concern prompts sympathy and comfort leads to empathy, care should result in ministry.

Care is an outward response to the sympathy and empathy of the heart. Specific action expresses concern and comfort. A Christian woman who recognizes a need in another and empathizes personally should be motivated to help through practical ministry. A single mother can offer assistance with childcare. A career woman can prepare a meal for a colleague stressed by impending deadlines. And a widow can wash clothes for a friend who has just lost her husband. In these tangible ways, a Christian is allowing her own suffering to be used by God for the sake of others.

In Romans 12:9-16, Paul the apostle challenged Christians not just to be concerned or extend comfort to those who are hurting, Christians should minister to them in love. **Read Romans 12:9–16, then list below several words or phrases that teach how to use personal suffering in ministry to others.**

The biblical teachings are clear—suffering can be for their sake. Ministry to others begins with genuine love (Romans 12:9). Christians can abhor or hate the suffering or pain, but trust that God will bring something good from it (Romans 8:28). We are to be kind and considerate to others, putting their needs before our own (Romans 12:10). We are to be diligent and dedicated as we serve the Lord and minister to others (12:11). We can have hope and joy as we persevere through tribulation (12:12). We are to give to others and show hospitality at all times (12:13).

In our suffering, we are to bless and not curse our offenders (12:14). Our attitudes of forgiveness and love will be a powerful testimony to others who are suffering. We are to join in celebration with those who rejoice and in weeping with those who mourn (12:15). Unity, humility, and wisdom from God are to be shared with others (12:16). We can rejoice when our own suffering results in ministry to others. My precious father-in-law, who served as a funeral director for 43 years, wisely told me, "Joy shared is multiplied; sorrow shared is divided." How true! It is God's desire that other people can be helped by our suffering.

You can rejoice in your times of hurt and pain knowing that "joy comes in the morning" (Psalm 30:5). For the Christian there can be joy in desolation (see Habakkuk 3:17–19). Claim those promises of God and share them with others as you suffer for His sake, suffer for your sake, and suffer for their sake.

 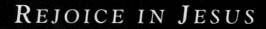

Philippians 2:5–18

The greatest joy of the Christian faith comes from a personal encounter with Jesus Christ. Believers can know God not only as Creator and Ruler, but trust Him as Savior and Lord. That personal commitment to salvation begins an intimate, long-term relationship with Jesus, who the Bible says is God in the flesh (John 1:14). Let's celebrate our salvation as we understand *who* Jesus is and *what* He has done for us.

Philippians chapter two contains one of four New Testament passages that explain Christ. **Before we examine these Scriptures, briefly describe who you think Christ is.**

Now read Philippians 2:5–11 to see how God explains His Son Jesus Christ. Based on this Scripture, answer the following question: who is Jesus Christ?

Paul attempted to explain to the Christians in Philippi the nature of Christ. His explanation helps us today. Christ is fully God and He is fully man. He left heaven and came to earth as a man to provide for our salvation. To His divine nature, He added a perfect human nature. He lived and worked among the people. He died on the cross, taking upon Himself our sins, so that we might be saved. He was raised from the dead and now reigns in heaven. This biblical doctrine is known as "incarnation." God became human. Divinity and humanity were united in Jesus of Nazareth, the promised Messiah, the Savior of the world.

It is essential for Christians to understand who Christ is and what He has done for us. The study of Christ's nature and person is called "Christology." It is another important biblical doctrine. What a Christian believes about Christ will affect other doctrines of the faith. While it is impossible to fully comprehend who Christ is, it is extremely important for evangelical Christians to accept the following truths about Christ:

- The reality of His two natures: He is both God and man
- The integrity of His two natures: they are not contradictory
- The unmingled union of these two natures in one: each nature is independent of the other (*The Woman's Study Bible*, 1952)

Do you believe these truths about Jesus Christ? How can you explain these beliefs to other people? Try to summarize your thoughts in simple language.

The *reality* of His two natures:

The *integrity* of His two natures:

The *union* of His two natures:

Throughout history, skeptics have doubted the incarnation of Christ. Even today, many unbelievers feel that Jesus was just a prophet or a good man. The Bible clarifies all confusion—Jesus Christ is truly God, with total deity, and truly man, with full humanity (John 1:14; Acts 17:3; Hebrews 2:14).

In this lesson we will examine key Christological passages to better understand the nature of Jesus. Try to carefully study these Scriptures to understand this foundational doctrine. You will have cause to rejoice as you learn more about Jesus—He is God, He is man, He is Savior!

HE IS GOD

Paul begins his discussion about Christ with a statement of His divinity: Jesus Christ is God (Philippians 2:6). Since that definition is based on knowledge of God, maybe we should first answer the question, "Who is God?" There is only one God, and He is Creator, Redeemer, and Ruler of the universe. A thorough description of God is found in "The Baptist Faith and Message" (adopted June 14, 2000), the confession of faith for Southern Baptists.

"There is one and only one living and true God. He is an intelligent, spiritual, and personal Being, the Creator, Redeemer, Preserver, and Ruler of the universe. God is infinite in holiness and all other perfections. God is all powerful and all knowing; and His perfect knowledge extends to all things, past, present, and future, including the future decisions of His free creatures. To Him we owe the highest love, reverence, and obedience. The eternal triune God reveals Himself to us as Father, Son, and Holy Spirit, with distinct personal attributes, but without division of nature, essence, or being."

What a profound statement of our belief in God! **Carefully reread the statement above, then list at least ten words that describe the nature of God.**

Because God is divine and we are not, we owe Him our highest love, reverence, and obedience. We must also understand that Christ is God. Read the doctrine of Christ that is generally accepted and believed by Southern Baptists ("The Baptist Faith and Message," 2000).

"Christ is the eternal Son of God. In His incarnation as Jesus Christ He was conceived of the Holy Spirit and born of the virgin Mary. Jesus perfectly revealed and did the will of God, taking upon Himself human nature with its demands and necessities and identifying Himself completely with mankind yet without sin. He honored the divine law by His personal obedience, and in His substitutionary death on the cross He made provision for the redemption of men from sin. He was raised from the dead with a glorified body and appeared to His disciples as the person who was with them before His crucifixion. He ascended into heaven and is now exalted at the right hand of God where He is the One Mediator, fully God, fully man, in whose Person is effected the reconciliation between God and man. He will return in power and glory to judge the world and to consummate His redemptive mission. He now dwells in all believers as the living and ever present Lord."

After you read the statement above, fill in the blanks to explain that Jesus Christ is God.

Christ is the eternal _____ _____ _____.

Jesus perfectly revealed and did the _____ _____ _____.

Jesus ascended into heaven and is now exalted at the _____ _____ ____ _____.

He is the One Mediator, fully _____, fully man.

In another letter to Christians in the early church, Paul wrote about the nature of Jesus. It is the second key Christological passage. **Read Colossians 1:15–18. How is Christ described?**

Christ is the image of God, the very likeness of Him (verse 15). He is the firstborn, the One who existed before all others (verse 15). He is the Creator of all things (verse 16). He is eternal (verse 17) and the head of the church (verse 18). Jesus Christ is fully God and fully man (Colossians 1:19; 2:9).

In order to complete our understanding of God, read the doctrine of the Holy Spirit from "The Baptist Faith and Message."

"The Holy Spirit is the Spirit of God, fully divine. He inspired holy men of old to write the Scriptures. Through illumination He enables men to understand truth. He exalts Christ. He convicts men of sin, of righteousness, and of judgment. He calls men to the Saviour, and effects regeneration. At the moment of regeneration He baptizes every believer into the Body of Christ. He cultivates Christian character, comforts believers, and bestows the spiritual gifts by which they serve God through His church. He seals the believer unto the day of final redemption. His presence in the Christian is the guarantee that God will bring the believer into the fullness of the stature of Christ. He enlightens and empowers the believer and the church in worship, evangelism, and service."

Christians today can rejoice because God is Father, Son, and Holy Spirit. Each attribute is distinct, though there is no division of nature, essence, or being. This divine mystery is beyond our human understanding and must be accepted by faith through biblical revelation. While the theological term "trinity" does not appear in the Bible, its truth is communicated throughout the New Testament. We can be joyful when we believe that Jesus is God and Jesus is Man.

HE IS MAN

Paul explained the humanity of Christ when he said that He took "the form of a bondservant," He came "in the likeness of men," and He was found "in appearance as a man" (Philippians 2:7–8). God the Creator became God in the flesh. The same God who made man in His likeness (Genesis 1:26) voluntarily made Himself in the likeness of man. God humbled Himself as He stepped down from His throne in heaven to live on the earth as a man.

Why do you think that God chose to become man?

The Bible says that God humbled Himself and became man—Jesus Christ. Christ was obedient to God's will, even to the point of death on the cross. He died in our place so that we could be saved. God became the man Jesus Christ because of His love for us and because of His desire to obey His Heavenly Father.

Now let's study a third key Christological passage. It also teaches that Jesus Christ is fully God and fully man. **Read John 1:14–18 and see how God ("the Word"—John 1:1) became flesh. How did John the Baptist respond when Christ began His ministry?**

John the Baptist, who had foretold the coming of Jesus, confirmed that He was the "only begotten Son of God" (John 1:18).

God became flesh—He was born as a man. To His divine nature He added a perfect human nature. Jesus Christ was conceived by the Holy Spirit and born of the virgin Mary. He was raised in the home of Mary and Joseph, then ministered for some years on the earth. Each of the four

Gospels records the life and death of Jesus—God who became man also died a human death and returned to His heavenly state.

Review one of the Gospel accounts of Jesus' time on earth and summarize some highlights of His life as a man.

In fulfillment of the prophecies of the Old Testament, Jesus was born in Bethlehem and grew up in Nazareth (Matthew 2:1, 23). He was baptized by John the Baptist in the Jordan River (Matthew 3:13; Mark 1:9; Luke 3:21). He was tempted by Satan but overcame the evil one (Matthew 4:1–11). Then He began His ministry in Galilee (Matthew 4:12–17). He trained twelve disciples who worked with Him (Matthew 4:18–22). For three years He taught parables, preached sermons, and performed miracles. Many people followed Him faithfully and helped Him expand His Kingdom.

To accomplish God's plan, Jesus was arrested, convicted, and crucified (Matthew 17:22–23). He died on the cross, was buried in a tomb, then rose from the dead on the third day in fulfillment of Scripture (Matthew 27–28). God came to earth as man to die for us. His brief time on the earth served a great purpose—He provided for our salvation. We can rejoice that Christ is God—He created us. We can rejoice that Christ is Man—He revealed Himself to us. We can rejoice that Christ is Savior—He redeemed us.

HE IS SAVIOR

The final focus of Philippians 2:5–18 is on Jesus Christ as Savior. God who became Man humbled Himself to the point of death on the cross. And at the name of Jesus "every knee should bow" (Philippians 2:10). Every tongue should confess that "Jesus Christ is Lord" (Philippians 2:11). Salvation is offered to all by faith in Jesus Christ.

In Philippians 2:11, three different names are used for God. **Read the Scriptures below and describe the meaning of each name.**

Jesus (Acts 2:22)—

Christ (Acts 2:31)—

Lord (Acts 2:36)—

God was given the earthly name Jesus, which literally means "salvation" (Luke 1:31). His messianic title or intercessory name was Christ (Acts 2:31). And Lord is His glorious eternal title (Acts 2:36; *The Woman's Study Bible*, 1979). Christians can relate personally to each name because Jesus is our Savior, the promised Christ, and our eternal Lord.

Now we should examine the fourth key Christological passage in Hebrews 1:1–4. **Read this Scripture carefully and identify three of the ways that God reveals Himself. Write them below.**

1.

2.

3.

The Bible, which is God's revelation of Himself to man, teaches that He has spoken at many times and in many ways. He has revealed Himself to the fathers, as He did with Moses in the burning bush (Exodus 3:2). He has revealed Himself through the prophets, like Isaiah and Daniel. But God's ultimate revelation of Himself to man was in His Son, Jesus Christ (Hebrews 1:2). The revelation that God gave through Christ is superior to all earlier revelations.

Hebrews 1 also affirms the total deity and total humanity of Christ. Jesus Christ is:
• appointed heir of all things
• creator of the worlds
• the express image of God
• all powerful
• purger of sins
• seated at the right hand of God
• higher than the angels
• a more excellent name

Jesus Christ is not only Savior of the world; He is my personal Savior. If anyone believes in Him, salvation is available by faith alone.

Have you been saved? Is Jesus Christ your Savior? Write a brief testimony of your salvation experience.

If you have been saved, then you can rejoice that Jesus Christ is Savior. I can rejoice! Jesus Christ has been my Savior since I was only 6 1/2 years old. At that time, in a childlike way, I understood that I was a sinner. I repented of my sin. I accepted the forgiveness of Jesus, and I completely trusted in Him. I was saved. I continue to rejoice in my salvation as I grow in my faith and serve the Lord.

What does it mean to us today that Jesus Christ is God, Man, and Savior? There is profound personal meaning to these biblical truths. If you believe in Jesus Christ, you can be saved, you can serve Him, and you can spread the gospel. It is not enough for Christians to rejoice in Christ. We must accept Him, we must serve Him, and we must speak of Him.

Philippians 2:19–30

In his letter to the Philippian Christians, Paul expressed his own needs and encouraged others to face their needs. He strengthened the church and strengthened his own ministry. He clarified truths and answered difficult questions. He emphasized humility in the Christian life and promoted unity among believers. He began with a sincere greeting and continued with heartfelt thanksgiving. He stressed commitment to the Lord and spreading of the gospel. He acknowledged inevitable life suffering but taught others to rejoice. In a key passage, Paul clearly described the nature of Christ. Throughout this book his theme was joy. Christians can rejoice because God is in control. Christians can rejoice because God can redeem any circumstance. And Christians can help other people rejoice. The Lord wants us to rejoice with others.

The last two verses of the previous passage begin Paul's call to Christians to rejoice with others. He said, "I am glad and rejoice with you all. For the same reason you also be glad and rejoice with me" (Philippians 2:17–18). Because the Philippian Christians knew of Paul's situation (imprisonment for his faith), their natural responses were concern and worry. They feared for his safety and wondered about his conditions. How reassuring for them to hear from Paul himself and be encouraged personally by him. He was okay. In fact, Paul said he was glad. He was joyful even in difficult surroundings. Then Paul asked his Christian friends to rejoice with him. **Who can you rejoice with at this time even though they are facing trials and tribulations?**

Why?

It is also important to understand why Christians can rejoice with others. **Take a few minutes to reread the first part of Philippians 2:17. Why could Paul rejoice with other believers?**

How did he rejoice?

The Bible says that Paul was "being poured out as a drink offering on the sacrifice and service of your faith" (Philippians 2:17). Paul had suffered for the sake of the gospel. He had willingly sacrificed his freedom in order to defend his faith. A "drink offering" was a particular type of sacrifice in Old Testament times. **Read about a drink offering in Numbers 15:1-16. Who was blessed by the drink offering given by Moses (see verses 15–16)?**

While an offering directly benefits the one who sacrifices, it is also a provision for others—"one ordinance shall be for you of the assembly and for the stranger who dwells with you" (verse 15). Paul's sacrifice not only covered himself but provided for others. Today we sacrifice ourselves and our own wills to the Lord, which blesses us and encourages others. We are to share our joys and sorrows with others so that all of us will grow stronger. We can rejoice with others as we rejoice in our own blessings.

In this lesson, we will focus on rejoicing with others. **Read Philippians 2:19–30. Who does Paul commend?**

How does he praise them?

What exactly does he say about their lives and ministries?

Paul often mentioned co-laborers in the faith in his letters. In this letter to the Philippians he gratefully acknowledged both Timothy and Epaphroditus. He listed both of them as representatives to his Christian friends in Philippi. He recommended them highly as faithful servants of godly character who would minister to the Philippians as they had ministered unselfishly to Paul. In this portion of his letter, Paul focused on the care needed by others, not himself. This lesson will consider how we can rejoice with others as we encourage them, support them, and esteem them.

ENCOURAGE OTHERS

Paul sent a messenger, Timothy, to visit his friends in Philippi. He wanted Timothy to encourage them and then return to encourage him. Before we consider this next passage, remember Timothy. **Who was Timothy?**

Read 1 Timothy 1:2 and 2 Timothy 1:2–7. What does Paul say about Timothy?

Timothy, who was from a godly family, was a faithful follower of Christ and like a son to Paul. He had ministered with Paul in Macedonia, Achaia, and Greece during the second missionary journey (Acts 15:39–18:22) and in Asia and Greece during the third missionary journey (Acts 18:23–21:17). Timothy grew in the Lord as he was mentored by Paul and had a significant ministry, often representing Paul to early Christian churches. Timothy was obviously close to Paul and cared for him deeply. He was sent to Philippi to nurture the missionaries there.

Paul sent Timothy to the Philippians to encourage them and in turn encourage him. **Read Philippians 2:19–24. How do you think Timothy encouraged Paul?**

How did he encourage the Philippian Christians?

Timothy learned directly from Paul how to be an encourager. When Paul was imprisoned and persecuted, Timothy was able to encourage his mentor, the one who had taught him about the Christian life. Paul acknowledged that he was cared for by Timothy, who unselfishly poured himself into ministry to him. His many acts of kindness as well as words of encouragement were greatly appreciated by Paul.

Paul often taught about encouragement or exhortation, a gift of the Holy Spirit. In a time of great persecution, Christians needed to be encouraged. But in any circumstances, people are strengthened by words of encouragement and acts of kindness. **Read Ephesians 4:25–32. How does Paul suggest that Christians should treat each other? List some key words or phrases of instruction below.**

The Lord had taught Paul how to unselfishly love and tenderly care for other people. He in turn taught others and us to speak in love, to not be angry, to edify and encourage, to be kind and tender, and to forgive as Christ forgave. In fact, our interaction with others, believers and unbelievers, should always be modeled after the care of Jesus for us. Paul continued that teaching in Ephesians 5:1–2: "Therefore be imitators of God as dear children. And walk in love, as Christ also has loved us and given Himself for us, an offering and a sacrifice to God for a sweet-smelling aroma."

Christians today are to love and encourage others, whether saved or unsaved. **Reflect for a few minutes on ways that you can encourage other people. What specific acts of love and kindness have you shared with others this past week? List several of them below.**

1.

2.

3.

Who **do you know that needs encouragement and** ***how*** **can you encourage them in the near future? Write your answers below.**

Who?   **How?**

Now pray this prayer aloud: "Lord, let me walk in love so that my words and actions will be a sweet smelling aroma to all those I know."

My dear friend Janet Hoffman, who is National WMU President, is such an encourager. Her sweet smile and gentle spirit convey such warmth and love. Her spoken words and written words affirm worth and work. Janet often writes me notes of encouragement. She may send a newspaper article about me or let me know she was blessed by my Bible study. And every time I see her, she gives me a great big hug. This lovely, petite lady is one of my strongest, most powerful encouragers. Don't you thank God for people like Janet? They lift us up and give us great joy.

Christians can rejoice with others as they encourage them and care for them. It is God's plan for those who minister to bless others and receive a blessing in return. Paul could rejoice with his Christian friends as he encouraged them in their faith. He taught Timothy and countless others to be encouragers. He also taught them by example not to simply encourage with words but to support others by meeting their specific needs.

SUPPORT OTHERS

In this section of Philippians 2, Paul mentions another friend, Epaphroditus. (My husband calls him "Eppie" for short.) He provided support to Paul and was to also support the Christians in Philippi. **Read Philippians 2:25–30 to learn about this friend in ministry. Who was Epaphroditus?**

How did he support other Christians?

Paul talked about Epaphroditus very fondly. He called him brother, fellow worker, fellow soldier, messenger, and minister (Philippians 2:25). He was obviously Paul's friend as well as a co-laborer in the faith. Epaphroditus had become seriously ill while in Rome with Paul. After his recovery, he wanted to return to his Christian friends in Philippi. He did so with Paul's blessing. In fact, Paul asked the Philippians to receive Epaphroditus in the Lord "with all gladness" (Philippians 2:29). Though Paul would surely miss his friend's presence, he rejoiced over his reunion with other Christians. Paul knew that Epaphroditus would be a strong support for the Philippians as he had been to him.

Epaphroditus almost lost his life as a result of his sacrificial service to Paul. **Have you heard similar missionary testimonies?** Many dedicated Christians leave the security of home to serve the Lord unselfishly in foreign countries. They often suffer, but they do so in order to serve others. Missionaries have often sacrificed their own health in order to help others. They often experience inconveniences in order to assist others. They often do without their basic needs in order to give to others. God calls us to support others sacrificially.

My husband and I are eternally grateful for many faculty and staff at the New Orleans Baptist Theological Seminary who sacrifice personally to support us in our ministry here. They could live in bigger houses, make more money, and achieve acclaim in other work, but they choose to serve the Lord here and support the work of others. How humbling! The work of the kingdom requires all Christians. We must support each other in life and ministry.

Paul often talked about the support of Christians to others. **Read 1 Thessalonians 3:6–10. How did Timothy support Paul?**

How can you support others?

Timothy had been a faithful coworker with Paul. He had returned to Thessalonica to see their Christian friends, and he was able to report their status to Paul. Paul was overjoyed to hear from Timothy that the Thessalonians were persevering in their faith. Their faithfulness was an encouragement to Paul as he faced his own trials. Timothy and other Christians supported Paul; they provided for his physical, mental, and spiritual needs. We are to support others, too. We can encourage them, support them, and esteem them.

ESTEEM OTHERS

In Philippians 2:19–30, Paul teaches Christians to rejoice with others as we encourage them (verse 19), support them (verse 25), and esteem them (verse 29). Paul praised Epaphroditus for his faithful service and asked the Philippians to receive him "with all gladness" and hold him in esteem. What a tribute to Epaphroditus! Paul felt he should be honored.

Take a few minutes to consider what Paul was asking the Christians in Philippi to do. What does the word "esteem" mean?

Webster's Dictionary defines "esteem" in this way: "the regard in which one is held; high regard, worth, value, regard." Christians are to value all people. But Paul felt extra recognition should go to Epaphroditus because of his sacrificial support—"because for the work of Christ he came close to death, not regarding his life, to supply what was lacking in your service toward me" (Philippians 2:30).

How did Paul suggest that the Philippians esteem Epaphroditus?

Paul asked them to accept him, acknowledge his service, and affirm his efforts. He had given his all for the sake of the gospel. Therefore, he was worthy of respect.

Do you know Christians who deserve the recognition and admiration of others? Many Christian leaders who serve faithfully are worthy of our esteem. We can look up to them and aspire to be like them, not because of their own human efforts, but because of the work of the Holy Spirit in their lives. God wants us to receive the esteem of others so that He can be glorified.

I am thankful that God has placed many godly people in my life that I can truly esteem. Their worth and work are examples for me personally. I highly esteem my husband, Chuck. He is a devoted man who humbly serves the Lord with all his heart. I also esteem many Christian women. I respect those who faithfully seek God and consistently minister in His name. I admire godly wives and mothers who support and strengthen their families. And I regard those who unselfishly go to remote mission fields to spread the gospel. God wants us to esteem others so that we will find joy in modeling their godly lives.

Later, in another letter, Paul encouraged Christians to esteem those who labored for the Lord.

Read 1 Thessalonians 5:12–19. How can you esteem others?

Paul was specific in this passage. He not only challenged Christians to esteem those who serve the Lord, but he told them and us how to esteem others. Recognize their work, respect their authority, and respond to their instructions. Esteem them very highly in love and be at peace. Admonish the unruly, comfort the weak, and be patient with all. Pursue what is good and not evil. What a big order! To esteem others involves unselfish love and personal sacrifice.

In 1 Thessalonians 5:16–18, Paul gave three specific instructions for rejoicing. **Reread those verses and fill in the blanks below to describe how to rejoice with others.**

* rejoice _____
* _____ without ceasing
* in _____ give thanks

How wonderful to know that as Christians we can rejoice *always*, *pray* without ceasing, and give thanks in *everything*. Now we must do it! Be determined to rejoice with others as you encourage them, support them, and esteem them.

Philippians 3:1–11

Paul begins chapter three of his letter to the Philippians with a passionate plea: "Finally, my brethren, rejoice in the Lord." At long last, after much discussion, Christians should rejoice. What a valuable life lesson! God wants us to experience abundant joy in life even if it takes a long time. He never gives up on us. He is patient as we seek His joy. Even when facing challenging circumstances, in time, we can rejoice in the Lord. Whether we feel joyful or not, He can help us rejoice.

Paul could rejoice in his circumstances not because good things always happened to him but because God was always with him. He learned to rejoice, then joy became his natural attitude. Why could Paul rejoice? Why can all Christians rejoice? **Read this week's focal passage—Philippians 3:1–11. Paul rejoiced not in who he was by birth but because of what God had done for him through rebirth. List below Paul's resume. What are seven of his personal credentials cited in verses 5–6?**

Paul thoroughly answered the question "who are you?" He identified himself as a true Jew—circumcised on the eighth day, born of the stock of Israel, specifically from the tribe of Benjamin, a Hebrew of Hebrews, a Pharisee committed to the law, a persecutor of the church, and blameless concerning the law (Philippians 3:5–6). Wow! What credentials! Paul built himself up so that he could explain that none of his credentials mattered.

His joy was not in himself, his background, or his accomplishments. His joy was in the Lord. His credentials were like rubbish! None of that mattered. His worth and his joy were found in Jesus Christ alone.

Who are you? Take a few moments to describe yourself. Think of who you are by birth and in life. Describe yourself with great accolades.

Now, remind yourself that none of that matters. Your connections and your credentials are like smelly garbage. They have absolutely no meaning compared to your worth in Christ.

I have a Ph.D. I am often introduced as Dr. Kelley. Before speaking, my resume is often shared with the audience. As I sit there and hear a list of my accomplishments, I am grateful for Christian parents who provided me with an excellent education and for a husband who encourages me in all of my professional and ministry pursuits, but to me, none of that matters. I don't see myself as Dr. Rhonda Kelley. I see myself as a redeemed child of God, forgiven and loved by my Creator, Savior, and Lord. That agrees with Paul's impression of himself. He said the only thing that matters is that he "may gain Christ and be found in Him"—that he receive "the righteousness which is from God by faith" (Philippians 3:8–9).

In this lesson we will learn how to rejoice not in who we are but who Christ is. We will learn to rejoice even when the circumstances around us are difficult. A faith-filled believer can be joyful in the Lord when facing false circumcision, difficult circumstances, or bad choices. Our joy is in Him!

FALSE CIRCUMCISION

Paul developed such a strong faith that he could rejoice even when facing adversaries and false teachers. In Philippians 3:2, Paul strongly warned all Christians to "beware of dogs, beware of evil workers, beware of the mutilation!" He was surrounded by people who proudly professed doctrines contrary to God's Word. We face similar false teachings today, so we must be on watch for them. We must listen carefully to their words, depend completely on the Holy Spirit, and cautiously compare their teachings to the Bible. Who were the false circumcision? Who are they today?

In the ancient Near East and in undeveloped nations today, dogs are often street roamers who scavenge for their survival. They live off of the remains of others. "Dogs" were not referring to beloved house pets. Jews often referred to Gentiles as "dogs." While the Jews had been carefully circumcised eight days after birth according to the law, the Judaizers or Jewish legalists who insisted on the rite of circumcision for all believers, Jews and

Gentiles alike, often ripped, tore, or mutilated tender new believers. They believed in error that conversion was a physical act of circumcision rather than the spiritual act of faith. Paul criticized them harshly and warned Christians of their errant practices. He contrasted them with the "true circumcision" who worship God in the Spirit, rejoice in Christ Jesus, and have no confidence in the flesh (Philippians 3:3).

Do you believe we encounter the "false circumcision" today? _____ Yes _____ No

If so, who are they?

What do they teach?

Why is it important to beware of them?

While it may be discouraging and confusing to live in a time of false teaching, Christians can still rejoice. God is sovereign and on His throne, ruling over our world today. His Word proclaims the truth, and it can be proclaimed confidently. The Holy Spirit inhabits His people, protecting us from evildoers, distinguishing between truth and untruth, and guiding our life decisions. Paul warned his Christian friends about the false teachers not only in Philippians, but also in Galatians. **Read Galatians 1:6–10. What was happening to many new converts?**

What truths of God's Word did the Christians need to remember when encountering false teachers?

How can Christians help new believers resist untrue doctrine?

Many new converts in Galatia were being led astray by false doctrine. The Judaizers were at work among immature Christians, trying to persuade them to add the law to their experience of faith. Naively, many followed the false teachers. Paul called their message "a different gospel" (Galatians 1:6). He contrasted it to the truth. Today, the gospel is perverted and Christians must beware. Paul foretold the consequences of false teaching in Galatians 1:8–9: "If we, or an angel from heaven, preach any other gospel to you than what we have preached to you, let him be accursed. . . . if anyone preaches any other gospel to you than what you have received, let him be accursed."

The consequences of perverting the gospel are clear and condemning. Anyone who preaches or teaches falsely will be accursed. The Greek word *anathema* is translated "accursed" and literally means "set aside for destruction" (*The Woman's Study Bible*, 1947). While false teachers may seem to succeed, God promised to judge them and condemn them to destruction. Christians are responsible to beware of false teaching and to warn other believers of untruth. God will then protect us against the false circumcision and the truth of His gospel will be proclaimed.

Christians can rejoice today that the gospel has been spread to many closed nations that were previously opposed to the truth. However, as countries become open to the gospel and allow missionaries to share the Word, those countries also become open to other religions and cults that are not grounded in truth. New believers must be discipled in the faith so that they will not be led astray by false teaching. My husband and I went to Russia on a mission trip several years ago. It was thrilling to meet many believers, to attend church publicly, and to use the Bible to teach English in the schools. God is doing a mighty work in that country. However, we learned that many new converts who were not growing in the faith and learning true doctrine were being proselytized by other religious groups. Mormon missionaries and Jehovah's Witness teachers have also targeted the country with their messages. Young believers are being confused by their false doctrine, which on the surface sounds similar to the Bible. Christians must be vigilant to resist untruth themselves and protect other believers from confusion.

Do you know anyone who has fallen away from the faith as a result of false teachers? _____

Write a prayer for him or her in the space provided. Ask God to draw that believer back to the truth of His Word.

Paul encouraged his Christian friends to rejoice even though they were surrounded by many who would speak against the truth. He challenges us today to have confidence in God. The truth of God will stand. He who is truth has always been and will always be. We can rejoice in that promise even when the wrong message of false teachers is proclaimed loudly. Rejoice in the truth when facing the false circumcision. You can also rejoice personally when you face difficult circumstances.

DIFFICULT CIRCUMSTANCES

It is often difficult to rejoice when we see the spread of false doctrine. It is also difficult to rejoice when facing difficult circumstances. Paul frequently called attention to his own hardships and struggles in order to teach Christians about the care of the Lord and the sufficiency of His grace. He repeated his testimony of suffering to the Philippians. **Read Philippians 3:7–11 very carefully. Try to compile a list of Paul's "losses" and "gains" as he followed Jesus. List them below.**

Losses   **Gains**

From a human perspective, Paul lost a lot when he was converted. He was a Jewish scholar, a religious leader, and a public persecutor before he met Jesus. In the world's view, he gave up everything to follow Jesus—position, power, prominence. Now he was facing persecution himself. But Paul counted all his personal accomplishments as loss and all his spiritual pursuits as gain. He truly experienced joy in his new life and in knowing truth.

In business, success is often measured in terms of loss or gain. The daily stock market reports describe the financial activity in terms of loss or gain. And even in our daily life we often explain what we have given up or received. When I left my career as a speech pathologist, my colleagues thought I had lost everything. They considered my call to full-time ministry to be forsaking my formal education, my professional position, and my lucrative salary. On the other hand, I knew that what seemed to be loss was truly gain as I sought to serve the Lord.

Difficult circumstances become divine callings when a Christian follows Christ. **In Philippians 3:7–11, find the words to complete the following statements of why we can have joy when facing difficult circumstances.**

- **I have counted loss for _____ (verse 7)**

- **for the excellence of the knowledge of _____ _____ my _____ (verse 8)**

- **that I may gain _____ (verse 8)**

- **be found in _____ (verse 9)**

- **through faith in _____ (verse 9)**

- **the righteousness which is from _____ by _____ (verse 9)**

- **that I may know the power of _____ _____ (verse 10)**

- **that I may know the fellowship of _____ _____ (v. 10)**

- **being conformed to _____ _____ (verse 10)**

The attitudes of Christians change when facing difficult circumstances. Loss becomes gain; despair becomes hope; sorrow becomes joy—all because of Jesus. When we focus on knowing Christ and experiencing His power, our attitudes become joyful. In this passage, Paul encouraged his Christian friends to grow in their knowledge of Jesus through Bible study and prayer. He urged them to know the power of Jesus as they walked with Him by faith. And Paul challenged them to fellowship in the sufferings of Christ.

Philippians 3:10 is an ideal Scripture to memorize and meditate on. Read that verse prayerfully then paraphrase it below.

Now commit this verse to memory. God will bring it to mind when you face difficult circumstances.

One way that Satan influences Christians is by discouraging us or making us feel helpless as we face overwhelming challenges. Paul faced the testing of the evil one and he rebuked him with confidence in God. He concluded that his righteousness was not his own or from the law, but "that which is through faith in Christ, the righteousness which is from God by faith" (Philippians 3:9). The joy that Paul experienced when he opposed the false circumcision and faced difficult circumstances can be ours, too. Christians can even rejoice after making bad choices, knowing that God redeems when we turn to Him.

BAD CHOICES

God created us in His likeness though our natures are human. He planned our lives though He gave us the power of choice. The God who loves us more than He loves Himself knows that we will often make bad choices. While we will experience the consequences of our bad choices, He is eager to forgive us and work through our lives again.

Earlier in his letter to the Philippians, Paul acknowledged the bad choices of his Christian friends. Because he loved them so much, Paul was concerned that they had chosen to live ungodly lives, disagree with other believers, and follow false teachings. They had made some bad choices. Their concerned friend reminded them of God's love and forgiveness. He challenged them to repent of their sins and return to God. He wanted them to focus on God and His will for their lives, not on themselves and their own wills.

Have you ever made some bad choices? Did you choose to follow your own will instead of God's way? In a spirit of repentance, summarize your disobedience in the space provided.

Every Christian has made bad choices. Unfortunately, some of us have made foolish decisions that have profoundly hurt our lives and those we love. A friend recently shared with me her burden for her teenage children. She herself had led a sinful, rebellious life before her conversion as a young adult. She continues to carry the guilt of her bad choices. Though she is a godly woman today, her past sin still haunts her. She prays desperately that her own children will never make the bad choices she did. Her heart's greatest desire is for them to live faithful, godly lives.

Paul was concerned about the bad choices of his Christian friends in Philippi.

Read Philippians 3:1–11 again and notice how Paul prayed for their wisdom and discernment. List several guidelines to be remembered when praying for good judgment.

Prayer can strengthen you and others as daily decisions are made. As we seek the mind of Christ, He will lead us and guide us. As we serve the Lord sacrificially, He will use us. As we submit to His will, He will conform us. God is exalted and glorified when His children are obedient and choose to follow His ways.

You can rejoice even when you have made bad choices. If you confess your sin and repent of your selfishness, God will forgive you and restore you to fellowship with Him (1 John 1:9). When your relationship with the Lord is broken by rebellion, there is great sorrow. But when that relationship is restored, there is great joy. You can experience true joy even as you face false circumcision, difficult circumstances, and bad choices because of the power of the Lord.

My life verse is my promise of joy—"Trust in the LORD with all your heart, and lean not on your own understanding; in all your ways acknowledge Him, and He shall direct your paths" (Proverbs 3:5–6). That can be your promise, too.

Philippians 3:12–16

Do you believe that God has a plan for your life? Do you think He has a work for you to do and a lifestyle to live? I do. The Bible says, "I know the plans that I have for you . . . plans for welfare and not calamity to give you a future and a hope" (Jeremiah 29:11 NASB). God knows and loves each one of us. He has a specific plan for our lives and our work. Christians can rejoice in knowing that God has a personal plan for them and can dedicate their lives to following that plan. One of the greatest challenges of the Christian life is understanding the will of God—clarifying God's particular plan and then doing it. Jeremiah the prophet explained how to find God's will after he stated the truth of God's plan.

Read Jeremiah 29:11–13. List below the six ways a believer is to learn about God's plans.

1.

2.

3.

4.

5.

6.

A believer can know the will of God, though at times it may seem difficult. God told Jeremiah to *call* on Him, *pray* to Him, *listen* to Him, *seek* Him, *find* Him, and *search for* Him. Persistence is necessary when searching for God's will. But if a Christian will pursue God, God will reveal His plans. A Christian can "miss it" without listening. God speaks His will and then we must follow.

Have you pursued God's will for your life in the past? Are you following His will at the present time? Are you seeking His plans for your future? Take a few minutes to consider the plans God has for you. At this time, what are God's plans for you in specific areas of your life? Write them below.

My life—

My work—

My ministry—

My family—

My future—

As you recorded God's plan for your life, you should have had cause for rejoicing. God loves you so much that He has a plan and a purpose for your life. His plan far exceeds your thoughts and dreams. His plans for you are perfect and will bring you great joy. According to the Lord Himself, His plans are for your best welfare so that you can have a future and a hope. He wants the best for you, but you must seek and follow His will.

My husband and I recently had the privilege of speaking for our nephew's high school graduation. We shared a message from this passage in Jeremiah with the graduates. The next week we faced a personal disappointment. Our long-awaited vacation trip to England was canceled at the last minute. As we grieved the loss of our trip, Chuck and I became confident in the plans God had for us. We had planned a wonderful vacation, but we knew that God had an even better plan. Sure enough, within hours, a new vacation plan developed—one that was relaxing and refreshing. As we reflected on God's precious provision, we realized that the graduation message had been for us.

Now read this lesson's Scripture passage in Philippians 3:12–16. Paul challenged the Christians in Philippi and he challenges us today to seek God's will. He made a lifelong commitment to pursue God's will so that he could "lay hold of that for which Christ Jesus has also laid hold of me" (Philippians 3:12). Paul determined that the "one thing" he should do as a faithful Christian was to follow Christ. **Have you made the same commitment? Yes _____ No _____. Are you seeking to follow God's plan for your life? Yes _____ No _____.**

You have probably heard many sermons and Bible studies from this passage. It is filled with powerful biblical teachings. In this lesson, we will identify three ways to pursue God's plan for your life so that you can rejoice. Like Paul, we must forget the past, reach ahead, and press upward. Make these actions the commitment of your heart and life.

FORGET THE PAST

In order to follow the will of God, Christians must forget the past. We must forget both our successes and failures. We must forget previous accomplishments and pursue His new plans. We must forgive our past sins and we must forsake our old ways. Though past memories cannot be totally erased, an obedient believer must no longer think about them. Past successes can lead to overconfidence, arrogance, or false expectations. Past failures can bring about poor self-esteem, lack of confidence, or false humility. While we can learn from our past mistakes, we are to move ahead in faith.

The Bible says that God forgives past sins if they are confessed: "If we confess our sins, He is faithful and just to forgive us our sins and to cleanse us from all unrighteousness" (1 John 1:9). Because of God's grace and mercy, He does forgive. Because of our sinful nature, we can't forget. God will help us forget the past.

Read the following Scriptures, then note what the Bible teaches about forgiveness.

Psalm 103:12—

Isaiah 1:18—

Micah 7:19—

Romans 3:25—

Hebrews 10:17—

The Bible teaches that God forgives all sin that is confessed. He removes it as far as the east is from the west (Psalm 103:12). While we may perceive an end to the directions north and south on a map or a globe, there is no end to east and west. God's forgiveness is unending. He washes away the scarlet sins of our past and they shall become pure as white snow (Isaiah 1:18). God casts out our sins and throws them deep into the sea (Micah 7:19). Our past is no longer visible. He passes over our sins and doesn't even see them (Romans 3:25). And God does not remember our sin—He forgets all that we have ever done wrong (Hebrews 10:17). What a cause for rejoicing!

In a recent chapel service at the New Orleans Baptist Theological Seminary, the speaker preached about the forgiveness of God and the forgiveness of man. He concluded that God can forgive and forget. He can truly remember sins no more. But humans, even Christians, can't really forget. The past is always a part of our memories. He challenged Christians to forgive and forsake. **What do you think that means? Briefly define the three words below.**

Forgive—

Forget—

Forsake—

Forgiveness is a voluntary act of the will. It means "to cease to feel resentment against" (Webster's Dictionary). God does not hold a grudge against us for sin that we have confessed. His forgiveness is "an act of grace to forget forever and not hold people of faith accountable for sins they confess" (Holman, 509). God can forgive and forget. Forsake means "to turn away from" (Webster's Dictionary). Christians can forgive their past sins with the help of the Holy Spirit and turn away from them. We should not revisit the past. Even though our past sins may be a part of our conscious memory, Christians should choose to forsake them.

An old time preacher said it this way: "God forgives our sin and He throws it into the sea of forgetfulness, then posts a sign saying, 'No fishin' here!'" How true! God forgives and forgets forever. He wants us to forgive and forsake. We shouldn't keep remembering our sin. Don't look back—look ahead.

Have you ever counseled a friend who has been hurt by someone they love? No matter how hard she tries, it seems almost impossible to forget what wrong has been done. I have had frequent opportunities to talk with hurting friends. My advice to them and my prayer for them is that they forget the past hurt and move ahead. God clearly commands us to forgive and forget. He does that for a specific reason—we will hurt ourselves if we cling bitterly to the past. A friend who is going through a divorce is developing great bitterness. She is having such a hard time forgetting what he did to her, forgetting what he said. While human pain is real, God promises forgiveness if we forget the past.

Paul believed he should forget the things behind and reach forward to the things ahead. As Christians seek to learn God's plans, we should stretch forward. Moving ahead is the only way for spiritual growth and is the only way to be in God's will. The Greek word for reaching is *epekteinomenos*, which vividly describes the way a racer runs hard for the tape at the finish line (Barclay, 66). The body is propelled forward by the total energy and effort of the runner. As we invest our efforts in the road ahead, we forget the obstacles and achievements of the past.

Paul presented the image of a runner who was focused only on the goal and was running toward it with all his energy. It is impossible to run forward if you are looking back. Make a commitment like Paul to forget the past and reach ahead. Focus on the future, not the past.

REACH AHEAD

Paul taught this principle in three ways in this brief passage. First, he said, "I press on, that I may lay hold of that for which Christ Jesus has also laid hold of me" (Philippians 3:12). Then he said he was "forgetting those things which are behind and reaching forward to those things which are ahead" (Philippians 3:13). Finally, he added, "I press toward the goal for the prize of the upward call of God in Christ Jesus" (Philippians 3:14). What a thorough explanation of how to reach ahead! Paul communicated clearly and consistently how Christians are to move forward.

The unsaved person is often controlled by the past, but the Christian should be focused on the future—life here on earth and an eternity in heaven with the Lord. An athlete or a businessman who keeps looking back will never succeed in the future. I read a sports story in the newspaper just yesterday of a track star who lost a national race by only 0.86 seconds when he looked back at his teammates. The reporter described his dejection when another runner won the prize because the track star paused to look back. We can lose the race of life if we keep looking back.

Let's examine three phrases in this passage that teach us how to reach ahead. In Philippians 3:12, Paul said, "I press on." In the next verse he said, "I reach forward" (3:13). And in the following verse, Paul said, "I press toward" (3:14). Though related, these three actions give different insights into how Christians should reach ahead.

Read Philippians 3:12–14 for yourself and determine what Paul is reaching ahead to receive. Identify the result in the verses for each action listed below.

Action   *Result*

"press on" (verse 12)

"reach forward" (verse 13)

"press toward" (verse 14)

71

The Christian can expect specific results when reaching ahead. First, we lay hold of Christ Jesus when we press on (Philippians 3:12). We understand more of Him as we seek to grow closer to Him. Second, we receive "those things which are ahead," the promises of God for our future (Philippians 3:13). Third, we achieve "the goal for the prize of the upward call of God in Christ Jesus" (Philippians 3:14).

Press on, *reach forward*, and *press toward* are all actions which require great effort. The Greek word translated "press" or "follow after" conveys great determination. The Greeks used the same word to describe the effort and eagerness of a hunter pursuing his prey. I can remember an occasion when I joined my teenage nephew in his deer stand. He was determined in his search for deer. He was patient to wait for the biggest buck even in the cold weather and uncomfortable structure. His efforts were worth it when he got his prize target.

You may be like me and fail to understand the passion of a hunter. You may be more passionate about shopping. Determination is needed by a shopper who is searching for a particular item or seeking the best bargain. Christians must learn to press forward.

Christians must be determined if we are to reach the goal. **What are some goals that you have set for yourself? What are your plans of action to accomplish those goals?**

Goal   **Action**

Your goals will never be accomplished without a plan of action. God has not only set a goal for you, but He has a means by which you can accomplish it. As you seek Him, He will reveal His ways. You can achieve the prize as you reach ahead—pressing onward and upward.

PRESS UPWARD

It is not surprising that Paul concluded this section by reminding Christians to press upward. In our endless pursuit of goals, we should always pursue God. As he reflected on his accomplishments and his challenges, Paul concluded that there was only one thing he should do. That one thing is to know Christ—press upward.

Jesus Christ Himself looked up to God His Heavenly Father. In the garden, He looked up as He prayed (Matthew 26:36–46). When He washed the feet of His disciples, He looked up in service to the Father (John 13:1–17). And even on the cross, Jesus looked up to His Father in obedience even to death (Matthew 27:45–56). If Jesus, the Son of God, turned to the Father, we should, too. Christians should press upward, looking to God for guidance and strength.

Later in the New Testament we are taught about looking upward to Jesus. **Read Hebrews 12:1–2. Now answer these questions:**

What should we lay aside?

How should we run?

Where should we look?

What is set before us?

Again the Bible uses the analogy of a race and a runner. As Christians we should run the race of faith like a skilled runner. First, we must lay aside every weight and any sin. It is essential to eliminate any stronghold that would restrict our movement. Sin or disobedience is certainly a heavy weight around the Christian, slowing down progress in the faith.

Second, we must run with endurance, persistence, and sustained effort. The Christian life is a marathon, not a 50-yard dash. We must be prepared to keep running and continue the faith all the days of our lives. Spiritual discipline and personal determination are required for the distance race of faith.

Third, we are to look to Jesus. While it is easy to be distracted by others, Christians should focus on the Lord. He is "the author and finisher of our faith" (Hebrews 12:2). He is the one who created us, redeemed us, and will claim us when He returns one day.

Finally, we should press upward for what is set before us. Jesus so wanted us to experience joy that He was willing to endure the cross and accept the shame so that He could accomplish our salvation according to God's plan. The same Jesus who died for us on the cross will return one day to claim us for His own.

Christians are to press upward. While it is often challenging to focus on the Father, we are encouraged by other faithful believers. The writer of

Hebrews reminds us that "we are surrounded by so great a cloud of witnesses" (Hebrews 12:1). The cloud of witnesses actually includes the faithful who have gone before us, preparing the way for us and strengthening us by example. The witnesses are not just passive spectators sitting up in heaven; instead they are active participants in the race of faith. They are cheering us on as we face life's challenges.

If you have not recently read Hebrews 11, read it now. It recalls the heroes of the faith, those who are our cloud of witnesses. List below the names of some of those godly examples.

How wonderful to know that Abraham, Sarah, Moses, and Rahab were among the faithful who have helped us press upward toward God. We can also look upward in anticipation of Jesus' return. The Bible promises that He will return one day to take His children to heaven. That is a great reason for rejoicing. In the meanwhile, we can rejoice in God's plan as we forget the past, reach ahead, and press upward.

Philippians 3:17–21

The Book of Philippians is filled with joy. Paul shared his reasons for rejoicing in this letter to the Christians in Philippi. However, he began to weep. As he concluded chapter three, Paul became emotional—concerned about the spiritual condition of his Christian friends. He was not burdened by his own circumstances. He was heartbroken over the way professed Christians were living. Many were continuing to follow the law and not live by grace. Paul was distressed that they were missing out on the joy of the Lord as they adhered to the letter of the law. His warning should also be heeded today.

Many new first-century converts were following the lead of false teachers or legalistic Jews. They were imitating the lives of the ungodly—Paul called them "enemies of the cross." They were confusing immature believers and facing peril themselves. Paul revealed his concern as he chastened them. He admonished the Christians in Philippi to follow his example of faith and walk the path of God.

Read Philippians 3:17–21. How does Paul describe the "enemies of the cross" in verse 19? Fill in the blanks below.

Their end is _____.

Their god is their _____.

Their glory is in their _____.

Their mind is set on _____ _____.

Paul's description of the sinners is clear. Their end is destruction. Their god is their belly. Their glory is in their shame. And their minds are set on earthly things. The mind, heart, and lives of sinners are focused on physical pleasures, which lead to destruction and death. Paul contrasted his own lifestyle of faithfulness to the sinner's lifestyle. He encouraged Christians to follow his godly lifestyle.

What should be the description of friends of the cross? Provide an opposite word in the blanks below.

Their end is _____.

Their god is their _____.

Their glory is in their _____.

Their mind is set on _____ _____.

Saints are friends of the cross who follow the Lord by faith and develop a different conduct. Their end is life because their God is the Lord and they nurture their spirits. Their glory is in their blessings and their mind is set on heavenly things. Paul was a positive example of godliness in his day. We can be a positive influence today.

Once Paul expressed his concern for their conditions, he provided reasons for their true faith. In one statement, Paul affirmed their worth and gave hope for the future—"our citizenship is in heaven." Earthly things have little heavenly relevance to us. We have the promise of heaven.

What do the following Scriptures teach about heaven? Read the verse and summarize its teaching. Then rejoice in the promise of heaven.

Matthew 6:9—

Matthew 11:25—

Luke 10:20—

John 14:2–3—

Acts 4:24—

2 Corinthians 5:1–2—

The Bible speaks often about heaven—the dwelling place of God our Father (Matthew 6:9). The Lord resides in and rules over heaven and earth (Matthew 11:25). Believers are recorded on the rolls of heaven (Luke 10:20), and Jesus is preparing a heavenly home for believers (John 14:2–3). God, who made heaven and earth (Acts 4:24), will one day call us home to heaven (2 Corinthians 5:1–2). What a precious promise! We have a mansion in heaven prepared by the Lord and waiting on us to spend the rest of eternity in the presence of God. We can rejoice in the promise of a place, of His presence, and of perfection!

THE PROMISE OF A PLACE

To His children, those who follow Him by faith, God promises a special place—heaven. While we are citizens of earth, as Christians, we are also citizens of heaven. We have dual citizenship—one temporal and the other eternal. Heaven is a real place where we will live after death for all eternity. What an amazing promise! What a great cause for rejoicing!

Let's think for a few minutes about dual citizenship. An individual with dual citizenship has identity in two countries at the same time. Privileges and responsibilities are experienced when citizenship is granted by birth or adoption. Some people today hold two passports because they have legal residences in both places. They enter and leave both countries freely and are obligated to obey the laws and pay taxes to both countries. A Christian is a resident of both earth and heaven. Earth is our temporary home, while heaven is our eternal home. Our permanent citizenship is in heaven. Our permanent address is heaven.

Citizenship is important today. Immigrants who come to America often dream of becoming a citizen of the United States. They work hard, learn the history and culture, and apply for citizenship. As the process concludes, they become naturalized citizens—not born in America but accepted here. Citizenship was vital in the Roman world of Paul's time. If people lived in a Roman colony, not just Rome itself, they could become citizens of Rome. The Philippians understood Paul's reference to citizenship because they knew the benefits of being citizens both of Philippi and of Rome. Though they received the daily benefits of life in the city of Philippi, they also received the privileges of Roman citizens. **Why do you think dual citizenship is important to Christians?**

The knowledge of dual citizenship gives the Christian the hope of heaven. When there are struggles and strife on earth, we have the promise of heaven to cling to. We know that earth and its hardships are only temporary. **Take a few minutes to write a description of heaven.**

Heaven is a place. I believe it is a real place where Christians will live in fellowship with God for all eternity. The Bible describes heaven in very vivid terms, but still it is impossible for the human mind to conceive the grandeur of heaven. John gave a glimpse of heaven in the Book of Revelation:

"Now I saw a new heaven and a new earth, for the first heaven and the first earth had passed away. Also there was no more sea. Then I, John, saw the holy city, New Jerusalem, coming down out of heaven from God, prepared as a bride adorned for her husband." —Revelation 21:1–2

The very thought of heaven is a cause of great rejoicing! John continued his picture of heaven in Revelation when he actually described its appearance: "The twelve gates were twelve pearls: each individual gate was of one pearl. And the street of the city was pure gold, like transparent glass" (Revelation 21:21). Heaven is the most beautiful place a human mind can envision, made of all the finest materials. Though we are unworthy, the God who loves us is preparing an amazing place just for us, His children.

I still remember vividly the wedding of Prince Charles of England and Princess Diana. It was celebrated throughout Britain and televised world-wide. The cathedral in London was exquisitely decorated with flowers, candles, ribbons, and carpets. The bridal party was beautifully dressed. It was truly a fairytale wedding, though there was no storybook ending to that marriage. However, the extravagant wedding in a resplendent church can only help us begin to imagine the glory of the place called heaven.

God is busy preparing a place for us. Jesus Himself said, "I go to prepare a place for you" (John 14:2). Everything in heaven will be new (Revelation 21:5). Won't that be wonderful! Our mansion in glory will be made just for us. It will be absolutely spectacular—designed specifically for us and brand new. Have you ever built a house or bought a new one? Though there are always some little kinks to work out, it is pristine—sparkling and beautiful. And besides, it is just for you. I remember well when my husband and I moved into the President's Home at New Orleans Baptist Theological Seminary on May 6, 1996. It was (and still is!) the loveliest home I had ever seen. And it was mine! Though it was almost 50 years old, it had been totally remodeled. It was a dream house. God is so good! But my beautiful home here on earth pales in comparison to the mansion God is preparing for me in glory. It will truly be my custom-built home, equipped with every convenience I will ever need for all eternity. And I am confident it will have a self-cleaning oven, no-wax floors, and guaranteed appliances. It certainly won't have pesky termites, chipping paint, or squeaky doors. Heaven is a perfect place for perfect people—God's children in their glorified states in the presence of God Himself forever. Wow! Heaven is a great cause for rejoicing!

THE PROMISE OF HIS PRESENCE

While believers are promised the presence of God through the Holy Spirit while living here on earth, we are promised to be present with God in heaven for all eternity. Paul clung to that hope throughout his life and ministry. He often wrote about heaven in his New Testament letters. Paul affirmed the truth that God was in heaven and believers will have fellowship with Him. In Ephesians 1:20 he said that God "seated [Christ] at His right hand in the heavenly places."

It is a fact that God reigns in heaven and that one day all His children will be at home with Him in heaven. Paul almost sounded homesick for heaven. **Have you ever been homesick? Have you ever been away from home and really missed your loved ones? Explain your feelings here.**

Homesickness is a longing in the heart to return home and be with family. It is a strong emotion that can impact all areas of life. I have been truly homesick on several occasions. I travel a lot and am often separated from my husband. I miss him terribly and am always eager to get home. There is no more beautiful sight to my eyes than our home. Seeing our house is a realization that I will also be seeing my sweetheart. I am most homesick when my travels take me overseas and the time changes even make phone conversations impossible. My deep feelings of longing for my husband should be a small taste of my homesickness for heaven and the presence of my Lord.

The promise of God's presence should encourage Christians to remain faithful and joyful until the day of the Lord. Simon Peter also anticipated heaven. He was eager to be with God. **Read 2 Peter 3:10–13. What does Peter say about heaven and the presence of God?**

Christians cannot be sure of when we will enter heaven. It will be either at the time of our death or when Jesus returns again. Both dates are unknown. Peter explained that we cannot know with certainty when He will come— The Lord will come "as a thief in the night" (2 Peter 3:10). But at our death or when He comes, we will immediately be with Him. We will dwell with Him in righteousness. We will be in the presence of God and godliness. Did you also know that we will be busy in heaven—busy about God's work?

79

Read the following Scriptures to identify some of our heavenly activities. What will we do in the presence of God?

2 Timothy 4:6-8—

2 Corinthians 5:10—

Romans 11:33–36—

1 Corinthians 6:2–3—

The Bible confirms that we will be very busy in heaven. Since we women are so busy here on earth, we will be prepared for activity in heaven. The first event on our schedule in heaven is an awards ceremony. As we enter heaven, faithful Christians will be rewarded (2 Timothy 4:6–8). We will receive crowns of rejoicing, righteousness, life, and glory, plus even more. (See 2 Corinthians 5:10; 1 Thessalonians 2:19; James 1:12; 1 Peter 5:4; and Revelation 2:10.) God Himself will award our crowns. What a privilege to receive rewards from our heavenly Father.

But that's not all. We will also be judged in heaven. While our godliness will be rewarded, our ungodliness will be punished. Our celestial celebration will be interrupted by the judgment of God. We will stand before the *bema* (judgment seat) to receive our impartial judgment, whether good or bad (2 Corinthians 5:10). What a relief to know that as Christians, our God is forgiving and He will never punish us in the way we truly deserve (Psalm 103:10–12). But knowledge of a judgment day should encourage obedience.

In heaven, we will also worship and praise God. We will spend all eternity giving glory to God (Romans 11:33–36). I can only imagine how exhilarating it will be to sing with the heavenly choir. My off-key voice will sound beautiful in heaven. We will also serve the Lord and rule over the earth with Him (1 Corinthians 6:2–3). How wonderful to know that we will spend eternity with God doing His work!

The Scripture also tells us that only believers will be in heaven. Not only will we be with God, but we will also be with His children. Just think of it—Christian fellowship for all eternity. There is nothing sweeter than fellowship with other believers.

Can you recall a recent time when you were greatly blessed by Christian fellowship? Describe your experience below.

It is always a joy to be reunited with Christian friends or to meet people who share a common faith in God. As I travel, I often meet Christian friends, and the fellowship with them is so uplifting. It is a joy to see many friends in ministry. We are blessed by the Christian fellowship.

While God has put us on the earth to be a witness to the unsaved, it is always a special treat to fellowship with the saved. We will also enjoy the presence of our saved loved ones. There is much mystery about our relationships in heaven. However, we can be confident that we will be present with our husbands, our parents, our children, our relatives, and our friends who are believers (1 John 3:2). That promise should also motivate us to share our faith with any of our unsaved family members or friends so that they, too, will spend eternity in heaven. Heaven is not just a promise of a place and His presence; it is a promise of perfection.

THE PROMISE OF PERFECTION

I do believe that one of the greatest promises about heaven is the promise of perfection. The Bible tells us that our bodies will be transformed into a perfect state. Paul said it so enthusiastically in Philippians 3:21: Jesus Christ "will transform our lowly body that it may be conformed to His glorious body." Wow! That is exciting. One day my worn-out old body will be changed into a glorious new body, fully like Jesus. All Christians can rejoice in that promise!

Jesus Christ was transformed into the likeness of His Father in an encounter with His disciples. **Choose one of these Gospel accounts and summarize in the space below the transfiguration of Jesus: Matthew 17:1–13; Mark 9:1–13; or Luke 9:28–36.**

What an experience for the disciples Peter, James, and John to see Jesus transformed into the image of God. He vividly predicted His death, resurrection, ascension, and return to glory. The sight of the transformed body of Jesus gave the disciples hope to face His death on the cross.

Jesus was transformed into a perfect divine state, and we will be transformed into His likeness. **Now read 1 John 3:1–3. Summarize the promise of perfection below.**

God, who has lavished His love upon us, has also promised that we will one day be like Him. John said it like this:

"It has not yet been revealed what we shall be, but we know that when He is revealed, we shall be like Him, for we shall see Him as He is. And everyone who has this hope in Him purifies himself, just as He is pure." —1 John 3:2–3

Though we don't know all the details about our heavenly appearance, we know we will be like Him—pure and spotless.

Joni Erickson Tada has spent about 30 years in a wheelchair as a quadriplegic. As a result of a diving accident, her body became damaged. Her faith has sustained her and given her a significant ministry. In one Bible study, she examines the promise of heaven (*Heaven: Your Real Home*). You can imagine how hopeful Joni is about heaven. She is eager to go to that special place and be in the presence of God. But she is truly excited about a glorified body. Her physically damaged body will be transformed into a perfectly formed body. All Christians can rejoice in that promise of heaven!

As we conclude this study of heaven, be reminded that only those who are saved will go to heaven. Jesus Himself said, "Unless one is born of water and the Spirit, he cannot enter the kingdom of God....You must be born again" (John 3:5, 7). As you anticipate heaven, be busy sharing your faith. It is God's deepest desire for all to be saved and receive the promise of heaven.

Philippians 4:1–7

As Paul came to the end of this letter to the Philippians, he remembered them personally and challenged them to pray. In chapter one, Paul greeted his co-laborers in the Lord and expressed joyful gratitude for their friendship (1:1–5). In chapter four, he repeats his greeting even more tenderly and with more concern—"Therefore, my beloved and longed-for brethren, my joy and crown, so stand fast in the Lord, beloved" (Philippians 4:1). Because of his deep love for the Christians in Philippi, Paul was very concerned about their wavering faith. He charged them to be faithful to the Lord, he identified some discord in the fellowship, and then he urged them to pray.

Paul specifically mentions two women in Philippians 4:2–3. While only little is known about Euodia and Syntyche, it is clear that they were grumbling. The two Christian women had been involved in building the church in Philippi. Paul recognized their diligent leadership in verse 3—"these women who labored with me in the gospel." However, their dispute was hurting the church and the cause of Christ. **Read Philippians 4:1–3. What two-fold recommendation did Paul make to unite the women and bring harmony to the church?**

1.

2.

First, Paul addressed the two women, calling them to "be of the same mind" (Philippians 4:2). He implored them (urged them passionately) to agree with each other. Petty grievances had come between them and it was hurting God's work. The ladies needed to unite around the gospel. Believers should always be yoked together for the cause of Christ. Paul then spoke to the church leaders and asked them to help Euodia and Syntyche reconcile. The body of Christ is to function in harmony. Often, church leaders can be used by God to bring peace to a troubled relationship. A healthy church is dependent upon healthy relationships within the congregation.

Is there any disharmony in your church at this time? If so, what is your role as a concerned Christian? How can God use you to bring about reconciliation and peace?

Much prayer is needed when quarrels develop in the church body. The parties involved must pray for wisdom and be willing to admit guilt. Church leaders must confront the situation and encourage repentance. Jesus told His disciples how to settle disputes between believers in Matthew 18:15–20. (You may want to read this passage now.) Several Christians are to go directly to the involved parties and help them resolve their differences. If friction continues, the whole church is to be informed. Paul was following the instruction of Jesus in trying to resolve the conflict within the church in Philippi. All believers must pray in one accord for peace to come to the broken relationship.

Prayer is a key to unity when division occurs between believers! Therefore, Paul quickly began a plea for prayer. **Now read Philippians 4:4–7. Based on this Scripture, what is your understanding of prayer? Write a brief description here.**

Prayer is communication with God—talking to Him and listening to Him. As we continue to examine this passage, we will discuss the priority of prayer, the prescription for prayer, and the promise of prayer. Prayer itself is great cause for rejoicing!

THE PRIORITY OF PRAYER

Prayer is an awesome privilege! It is such an honor to be able to talk to God, sharing deep feelings and needs. But with the privilege of prayer comes responsibility. We must do it! We must find time to pray. We must make prayer our number one priority. Paul understood the priority of prayer. While the Christians in Philippi were grumbling, Paul startled them to get their attention. He said, "be anxious for nothing." He meant—Stop! Stop right this minute! Do not worry about trivial matters! Your squabbling is unimportant! Cease your whining and complaining immediately and instead pray! Paul stressed the importance of prayer. Prayer should be our most important priority.

Most believers sincerely desire to spend time with God in prayer, though few actually do it. When Christians prioritize their prayer lives, they receive rich blessings. When we do not pray faithfully and fervently, we miss out on some of God's most precious blessings. Prayer is a spiritual discipline. It takes personal discipline to prioritize prayer. **Do you know someone who is truly a prayer warrior? Who?**

What blessings do you see her receive as she prays faithfully?

The Bible teaches us about the importance of prayer. In the book of Philippians, Paul says we are to pray about everything (Philippians 4:6). Even though God knows what we will say even before we pray, He still wants us to talk with Him. **What do these Scriptures teach about the priority of prayer? Write a brief answer from each reference.**

Psalm 46:10—

Psalm 55:17—

Luke 6:12—

Luke 18:1—

1 Thessalonians 5:17—

James 5:13—

Prayer should be a priority for every believer. We are to take time to be still and hear a word from God (Psalm 46:10). We should pray as David did, all day—morning, noon, and evening (Psalm 55:17). We should pray like

Jesus, for extended periods of time, especially if we are making important decisions (Luke 6:12). We must establish a definite time and place for prayer as we prioritize it in our daily schedules (Luke 18:1). We must pray without ceasing (1 Thessalonians 5:17), and we should always pray when facing challenges or trials (James 5:13). Prayer should be a priority for every Christian. We should pray at all times, when things are good and when things are bad.

Jesus Himself said that we are to "seek first the kingdom of God and His righteousness, and all these things shall be added to you" (Matthew 6:33). When we pray first and pray continually, God will provide for all our needs and pour out on us many blessings. Jesus, who prayed to the Father faithfully, taught His disciples to pray. In Matthew 6:9–13, He gave them a model prayer as an example. It is a step-by-step procedure for prayer. He also demonstrated through His life on earth the importance of prayer. The disciples often found Jesus praying. In fact, he frequently prayed for them. In John 17:6–19, Jesus prayed for His disciples very specifically. He prayed that they would remain faithful, that they would remain joyful, that they would remain safe, and that they would remain holy. His prayer for them is also for us today. Jesus teaches us to rejoice as we make prayer a priority.

How do you make prayer a priority in your life? What are some resources you use or procedures you follow to keep your prayer life meaningful? List them below.

There are so many resources on prayer available today. Books and Bible studies teach us about prayer and how to pray. Prayer journals and prayer lists can be used to record requests as well as responses. Focused times of prayer for missions as well as prayer walking can be effective tools for prayer. Several years ago I created a prayer basket. It is a wicker basket with a handle that holds my prayer resources. It has a devotional book on prayer, a slim-line Bible, a prayer journal, a pen, a highlighter, a notepad, notecards, and kleenex (for my tears). When it is prayer time, I can grab my prayer basket and immediately begin my time with the Lord. I have shared this prayer resource with my mother and mother-in-love, who use it faithfully as they pray.

There are many ways to pray, and there is no particular right time or right place. However, prayer needs to be an important part of every believer's life. Is prayer a priority in your life? Make a new commitment to prioritize prayer. When you focus on Him, God will give you cause for rejoicing! Now let's consider the prescription for prayer.

THE PRESCRIPTION FOR PRAYER

The Bible not only calls us to pray, but it guides us in prayer. Paul pleaded with his Christian friends in Philippi to turn to God in prayer and turn away from their personal conflicts. He taught them how to pray. He gave a specific prescription for prayer in this brief passage.

Reread Philippians 4:6 and discover what God teaches about prayer. Fill in the blanks below to complete this prescription for prayer.

in _____ pray

make s_____

with _____

let your _____ be known

to _____.

Paul makes it clear that prayer is not a difficult practice. It is a spiritual discipline that requires attention and energy. We are to pray scripturally and we are to pray specifically. These verses teach us to pray in *everything*. We should talk with God about every area of our lives and approach Him with every concern. No detail of our lives is too small for God to respond. In prayer, we are to make *supplication*. God wants us to communicate with Him and to share our hearts' desires. We should always pray with *thanksgiving*. We should express gratitude for who God is and what He does. We can be grateful that God hears and answers our prayers. According to this biblical prescription, we are to let our *requests* be made known to God. He is blessed when we talk with Him about specific concerns. And our prayers should always be directly addressed to *God*. We don't have to pray to someone else or through someone else. We can go directly to God in prayer.

There are several different words often used in the Bible and by Christians in reference to different kinds of prayers or different ways to pray. **Briefly describe your understanding of the following prayer terms.**

Supplication—

Request—

Intercession—

Petition—

While it is not necessary to over-analyze the meaning of these words or play the game of semantics, it is helpful to understand their meanings so we can learn more about prayer. The dictionary gives us a simple definition for each word, and we can adapt it to the process of prayer.

Supplication—"to ask for earnestly and humbly."

Request—"something asked for or sought after."

Intercession—"prayer, petition or request in favor of another."

Petition—"something asked for or requested."

Supplication can be viewed as general prayers for others or self. Christians may pray generally for the work of the church, the protection of family, or health of parents. God hears these general prayers and personalizes them. Requests can be seen as more specific prayers—particular needs of individuals. We can voice concern about the needs of others or ourselves. Intercession and petition often refer to the process of our prayers. Christians intercede to the Father on the behalf of others who have needs. We also petition or directly ask the Lord for our own needs. How wonderful to know God wants us to pray generally and specifically, for others and ourselves. He simply wants us to pray.

Have you been praying generally and specifically for others and yourself? Write below a recent prayer for each type of communication with God.

Supplication—

Request—

Intercession—

Petition—

Through the years, Christians have developed some misconceptions about prayer. God wants us to know the truth about prayer and its power. In her book *Live a Praying Life*, Jennifer Kennedy Dean suggests that there are four major misconceptions about prayer.
1. Prayer is only for material needs.
2. Prayer is to convince God to implement our ideas.
3. Prayer is to hold God to His promises.
4. Prayer helps pry riches out of God's reluctant hands.

These statements are not true. Do you recognize the false teaching? **Rewrite each statement in an accurate form.**

1.

2.

3.

4.

Myths about prayer can limit its power. Christians must recognize the fallacies and respond to the truth about prayer. Prayer is much more than requests for material needs. We don't pray to get things from God. We pray to know Him. And we make requests for every kind of need, not just material ones. In prayer we do not need to convince God to implement our ideas. Instead, we should seek to understand His plans. Prayer is not needed to hold God to His promises. He remembers His promises and will fulfill them in His time. Prayer does not pry riches out of God's reluctant hands. He freely gives out of His mercy and grace. The truth about prayer will give you great joy. God wants to unleash all of His promises about prayer in your life.

THE PROMISE OF PRAYER

Prayer is one way to know the promises of God. He will reveal His character and release His blessings as you pray. God has given to His children many precious promises (2 Peter 1:2–4). Through prayer you can understand and claim His promises.

God has actually made promises about prayer itself. The Old Testament prophet Jeremiah remembered God's promise of prayer. **Read Jeremiah 33:1–3. What is God's invitation to believers and what is His response?**

Invitation—

Response—

God extends a gracious invitation to all His children. He tells us to call on Him. Then He will answer. God's invitation to Jeremiah in the Old Testament has been extended to New Testament believers, too (John 15:16).

Take a few minutes to consider another "if-then" promise of God about prayer. Read 2 Chronicles 7:14. Identify the "if-then" conditions of prayer below.

If—

Then—

What do these two Old Testament passages teach you about the promise of prayer?

God's promise about prayer does have a condition. If God's people call on Him in prayer, then He will hear and answer. God cannot answer our prayers and fulfill His promises if we do not pray. In prayer we call on God, are convicted of our sins, and commit to righteous living.

What did Jesus teach His disciples about the promise of prayer? **Read John 14:13–14 below and underline the answer to this question.**

"Whatever you ask in My name, that I will do, that the Father may be glorified in the Son. If you ask anything in My name, I will do it."

God promises to *do* what we ask if we ask Him.

While God always answers our prayers, He does have different answers. Have you noticed that? Sometimes His answer is "yes." Sometimes His answer is "no." And often His answer is "wait." I am grateful that His answer is never "I don't know." Sometimes we ask according to God's will, so His answer is positive. Other times we ask selfishly, according to our own wills, so His answer is negative. And often His answer is "wait" so that His will can be fulfilled in His timing. God's response is always for our good because He is omniscient (all knowing).

Reflect on recent answers to your prayers. Give an example of God's response.

Yes—

No—

Wait—

Recently God clearly responded "yes" to our prayer for a relative's important decision. He definitely responded "no" to a new writing assignment I was considering. God has responded "wait" to my request for another women's ministry professor at the seminary. Even while waiting, I have trusted God's promise to hear and answer my prayers. I have learned to trust His answers, no matter what they are.

God has promised to respond to prayer. He has also promised to be present through prayer. One way for the believer to experience the presence of God is to spend time with Him in prayer. While waiting for heaven, we can spend time with God in prayer. From the time of our conversion, the presence of the Holy Spirit works in our lives as Helper, Tutor, and Guide (John 7:37–39; Acts 2:33).

God's promise of prayer is also for wisdom. As we seek Him, God will give us guidance and counsel. In fact, at times when we don't know how to pray or what to say, God gives us the words to pray (Romans 8:26). As we pray, He will help us know what to do and how to live. His promises about prayer are truly exceedingly great and precious (2 Peter 1:4).

In his letter to the Philippians, Paul underscored the importance of prayer. He had personally experienced the joy of prayer. Because he had prayed faithfully and effectively, God had answered his prayers. Paul knew that devotion in prayer had strengthened him and protected him. He closed this passage with these words: "And the peace of God, which surpasses all understanding, will guard your hearts and minds through Christ Jesus" (Philippians 4:7). God will always keep His promises about prayer. In that promise we can have peace and joy.

Philippians 4:8–9

As Paul continued to communicate his passionate concern and persuasive directives to his Christian friends in Philippi, he challenged them to focus on thinking godly thoughts, living godly lives, and doing godly deeds. Most people would agree that thoughts dictate actions—that what is in the mind usually comes out in the life.

Therefore, if a person thinks godly thoughts, she will be more likely to live a godly life and do godly deeds. On the other hand, if she thinks ungodly thoughts, she will usually live an ungodly life and do ungodly deeds. Paul wanted the Christians in Philippi to concentrate on their hearts and minds. God wants all of His children to contemplate only what is good, pure, and godly. In Isaiah 26:3, the prophet said that God would keep in perfect peace the one whose mind is stayed on Him. When we have God in our hearts and minds, we will evidence God in our lives and in our actions.

Through the inspiration of the Holy Spirit, Paul again wrote about godly virtues. It was no accident that he chose to list admirable traits recognized in Greek culture and taught by Jewish leaders. The Greeks sought truth and justice, while the Jews esteemed purity and goodness. These attributes admired by both Greeks and Jews are commendable, but it is important for Christians to live above and beyond others in the world. Our lives should never hinder the work of the Holy Spirit in the lives of unbelievers. Instead, our godliness should exceed the goodness in the world, bringing glory to God and drawing people to Him.

At this time, read our focal passage in Philippians 4:8–9. It would be helpful to read it in several different translations.

Now list on the next page the godly virtues that Paul tells us to meditate on in Philippians 4:8.

Now read several other passages from Paul's letters to understand his emphasis on godliness—Galatians 5:22–23 and Colossians 3:12–14. List the specific virtues from each passage in the space above.

Though the specific virtues vary in each letter, Paul stressed the importance of walking in the faith and living righteous lives. To the Philippians, Paul emphasized the virtues of truth, honor, justice, purity, loveliness, and excellence (Philippians 4:8). Those godly virtues will certainly set Christians apart in the world today. To the Galatians, Paul contrasted the fruit of the Holy Spirit with the sinfulness of human nature. Those who "walk in the Spirit" (Galatians 5:16) will be characterized by love, joy, peace, patience, kindness, goodness, faithfulness, gentleness, and self-control (Galatians 5:22–23). And to the Colossians, Paul suggested righteous clothing that is to be worn by all believers—tender mercies, kindness, humility, meekness, patience, forbearance, forgiveness, and love (Colossians 3:12–14).

These virtues cannot be lived out if they are not first thought about. The Bible says "as he thinks in his heart, so is he" (Proverbs 23:7). Christians today must think godly thoughts, then they can live godly lives. When sinful thoughts come to mind, they must be confessed and forsaken. Good and godly thoughts must replace them. Then Christians will be more consistent in living a godly life and doing godly deeds. Now, let's examine exactly what Paul taught the Christians in Philippi about their inward and outward behaviors. We can rejoice in our godliness, knowing that God will receive the glory.

THINK GODLY THOUGHTS

Paul moves toward the conclusion of his letter to the Philippians in verse 8 when he says "Finally, brethren." Once before in Philippians, Paul said "Finally, my brethren" (Philippians 3:1). But he paused to discuss several hallmarks of the Christian life first. Then in chapter four he summarized his ideas. He wanted to conclude with a positive recommendation to wavering Christians. He gave them a list of virtuous thoughts to meditate upon. You have listed the six virtues given by Paul. Now let's discuss them.

Write a brief description of each godly trait below.

True—

Noble—

Just—

Pure—

Lovely—

Good report—

Why do you think Paul selected these six virtues?

One more time Paul wanted the Philippians to give serious consideration to what they thought about and what they did. Each word was a unique Christian virtue to be pursued. Try to understand them as described below.

True—absolutely accurate, dependable
Noble—honest, honorable, respectable
Just—right, fair, impartial
Pure—moral, holy, righteous, without blemish
Lovely—attractive, appealing, lovable
Good report—excellent, sound

King David used many of these same words to describe God's Word in Psalm 19:7–9. **Read that Scripture to recall the authority of the Bible.**

Why do you think similar words are used to describe both the Word of God and His children?

It is the Bible that reveals the character of God and provides wisdom for His children to live godly lives (see Deuteronomy 29:29). The faithful study of God's Word helps the believer think godly thoughts, live a godly life, and do godly deeds.

Any godly virtue is worthy of consideration personally and worthy of commendation to others. Christians today should not only think godly thoughts themselves, but we should teach other Christians to think only the things of God. By example and through instruction, we can pass along a legacy of godly thinking. Future generations of Christians must learn to think pure thoughts.

Godly thoughts need to be a part of our deep conscious and subconscious minds. It is generally believed that thought patterns can become ingrained in a person's heart and mind. Let me relate a humorous example of this. Years ago, my husband had outpatient surgery. His youngest sister and I were sitting with him in the recovery room when he suddenly sat up in the hospital bed and began to recite the television schedule. In his groggy condition, he repeated: "at 7:00 P.M. on channel 6 *Sixty Minutes*, at 8:00 P.M. on channel 6 *Frasier*, at 9:00 P.M. on channel 8 *Dateline*," and so on. We were stunned. Later we discovered that Chuck had read *TV Guide* before he received anesthesia. What went into his mind before surgery came out his mouth in recovery. We have laughed about that through the years. But it has also been a serious reminder to us that what goes into the mind will usually come out in behavior or speech.

If you think about things that are true, noble, just, pure, lovely, and of good report, you are being an obedient child of God, you are enjoying blessings from God, and you are living a virtuous life for God. A virtuous life brings glory to God, not praise to a person. Christians should not be motivated to goodness for their own sakes but for God's sake. Since it's impossible for us to be godly in our own power, we can easily give the glory to God. It is wonderful to know that God works through a godly life to draw unbelievers to Himself. That is why we rejoice in our godly virtues.

LIVE GODLY LIVES

It is not enough to think godly thoughts. We must also live godly lives. Since it is difficult to separate godly attitudes from godly actions, we must seek to be godly in both our minds and lives. That is another recurring theme in the letters of Paul. In Colossians 3, Paul first charged Christians to "set your mind on things above" (verse 2), then he challenged them to "put on" godly virtues, to live godly lives (verses 12–14). Only then can the peace of God rule in your hearts (verse 15).

After his description of Christian virtues, Paul gave a formula for godly living. The things of God that you learn, receive, hear, see, and do will result in a godly life. **Complete the formula for godly living below from Philippians 4:9.**

_____ + _____ + _____ +

_____ + _____ = **godly life**

Each step is important in the process of godliness (sanctification). **Can you think of a synonym or word with the same meaning for each component of the formula? Write your own words this time.**

_____ + _____ + _____ +

_____ + _____ = **godly life**

A first step in the process of godliness is learning from God. We must understand how God teaches us to live and then do it day by day. Then we must receive His instructions. Not only do we receive Him by faith at salvation, but we continue to receive His guidance. We also hear Him; we perceive His general words and we become aware of His specific comments. Next we see Him—at work in His world and at work in His children. Finally, we must do what God tells us to do. We must obey Him. We must live godly lives. He says, "Do not be conformed to this world, but be transformed by the renewing of your mind" (Romans 12:2). So we must do it!

Paul used himself as an example of one who learns, receives, hears, and sees from the Lord and then does it. So he encouraged the Christians in Philippi to follow him—to imitate his example. As Christians we must follow the leader. Our leader is Jesus Christ. In Ephesians 5:1, Paul reminded us to "be imitators of God as dear children." We cannot simply love Him and trust Him; we must follow Him by faith. We become more like Him. We become godly. We begin to think godly thoughts and live godly lives. It is essential that we not take our eyes off the Leader. Focus on the Lord.

God gives us godly role models to follow. We can learn from the children's game "Follow the Leader." Christians are to play "Follow the Leader" with God as the permanent, perfect leader. Whatever He thinks, we are to think. Whatever He does, we are to do. Whatever He says, we are to say. If we practice, we can become champions at playing follow the Leader. If we don't practice, we will fail and we will look like ourselves, not God. We will be living ungodly lives.

In the same way that God brought Paul into the lives of the Christians in Philippi to model godly living, He brings godly people into our lives. **Can you think of several Christians who have been godly examples for you to follow? Write their names below.**

Take a moment to thank the Lord for them. But also be aware that there are other people who could be ungodly influences on you. Earlier in chapter 4 of Philippians, Paul warned the Christians about the disharmony between Euodia and Syntyche. Paul knew that human nature is such that other Christians would begin to quarrel because of the negative example of those ladies. He publicly acknowledged their ungodly behavior to warn their fellow believers, then he encouraged the truly godly to help them.

Recently, a well-known public figure was criticized for living an ungodly life. William Bennett, author of *The Book of Virtues*, admitted to a gambling problem. While he initially defended his innocent vice and his wife declared that his gambling days were over, the media debated the wickedness of gambling. How tragic for a respected "virtues maven" to live a hypocritical life! He was teaching godly living while living an ungodly life. Paul warned us about the same moral inconsistencies.

Do you know anyone who can be a bad influence on you? Certainly as we reflect on our childhoods or teenage years, we can remember friends that led us astray. But are there some people in your life now—at home, church, or work—who can rub off on you negatively? I have one friend who likes to talk about other people. What begins as innocent comments often turns into vicious gossip. I have to work hard not to contribute to the critical conversation. Whenever I am around her, I pray that God will help me to be like Him and not like her. I want to be consistently godly at all times and with all people.

In his letters to the Christians in Ephesus, Paul challenged them to live godly lives. **Read the following verses and identify the instruction for godly living.**

Ephesians 3:14—

Ephesians 4:1—

Ephesians 4:15—

Ephesians 4:22—

Ephesians 4:29—

Ephesians 5:1—

Ephesians 5:15—

Ephesians 6:10—

Ephesians 6:18—

The Bible does not just call us to live godly lives, it tells us how to do so. The Ephesians were taught to "bow the knee to the Father"—to pray for understanding and guidance (3:14). Christians are to "walk worthy of the calling" to salvation and service (4:1). We are to "speak the truth in love"— speaking only what is true and always with kindness (4:15). We are to "put off the old," laying aside our sinful former conduct to become godly (4:22), and "let no corrupt word proceed out of our mouth" (4:29). Christians are to always "be imitators of God" (5:1) and "walk circumspectly" or carefully (5:15). The Bible also instructs us to "be strong in the Lord and in the power of His might" and to "stand firm" in the faith and against evil forces (6:10, 14). We are to "pray always with all prayer and supplication in the Spirit" (6:18). Those are just some of God's guidelines for godly living. The Bible contains many more directives. But we must believe them and follow them. Then we can rejoice in our godly virtues!

DO GODLY DEEDS

As a believer develops a godly mind and a godly life, it is more natural to do godly deeds. Jesus, who thought pure thoughts and lived a godly life, also did godly deeds. There are many people in need who can be helped by our acts of kindness. We can rejoice as we live out our godly virtues.

It may be helpful to remember some good deeds of Jesus Christ. His life and ministry were filled with acts of kindness. **Read the following records of the unselfish works of Jesus, then summarize them briefly.**

Matthew 8:14–15—

Mark 5:35–42—

Luke 13:10–13—

John 2:1–11—

Each Gospel records the godly deeds of Jesus. Whenever He saw a need, He responded in kindness and love. Jesus healed Peter's sick mother-in-law and she arose to serve (Matthew 8:14–15). He raised Jarius' daughter from the dead and she began to walk (Mark 5:35–42). He healed the bent woman and she stood tall (Luke 13:10–13). And Jesus turned the water into wine at the wedding in Cana, and the people began to drink (John 2:1–11). These are only a few accounts of the good deeds of Jesus.

Many godly women of the Bible also did good deeds. They are examples to us of godly service. **Read the following passages then match each woman with her act of kindness.**

Godly Woman	Godly Deed
1. Rahab (Joshua 2:1–24)	a. sewed clothes for the widows
2. Esther (Esther 8:1–17)	b. served people in her home
3. Martha (John 12:1–2)	c. delivered the land into the hands of God's people
4. Dorcas (Acts 9:36–42)	d. shared Jesus with her household
5. Lydia (Acts 16:11–15)	e. saved her people from destruction

Godly people do godly deeds. The Bible confirms the goodness of God's people. Rahab the harlot was used by God to deliver the land into the hands of God's people (answer 1=c). Esther, the Jewish queen of Persia, was God's chosen one to save her people from destruction (answer 2=e). Martha of Bethany (the sister of Mary and Lazarus) served people faithfully in her home (answer 3=b). Dorcas, a devoted disciple, sewed clothes for the widows in Joppa (answer 4=a). And Lydia, a seller of purple, shared Jesus with her entire household (answer 5=d). Each woman was committed to the Lord and lived a godly life. Their godly deeds were a testimony of their inward and outward righteousness.

Christians are to always think and do what is good. However, we need not grow weary in doing good or in living godly lives (2 Thessalonians 3:13). Instead, we can experience peace from God and receive His abundant blessings. Paul concluded his letter to the Thessalonians with a reminder of this truth—"Now may the Lord of peace Himself give you peace always in every way" (2 Thessalonians 3:16).

The Bible teaches us that there are things to *think* (true, noble, just, pure, lovely, good things), there are things to *do* (learn, receive, hear, and see Him), and then there are things that happen to *you*. God promises to give you His peace. It is a promise to be given to and enjoyed by godly Christians.

Reread Philippians 4:9b. What is the verb in that phrase? "The God of peace _____ _____ with you."

Peace is a definite promise. It is not a probable dream. "Will be" is a verb of future tense with continual action. So we can be confident that our God who loves us will give us peace, and His peace will be experienced forever. That is definitely cause for rejoicing!

LESSON TWELVE   REJOICE ALWAYS

Philippians 4:10–23

In his closing verses to his friends in Philippi, Paul expressed his reasons for rejoicing. Even in his deepest despair and greatest need, Paul could be joyful because of the sufficiency of Christ and the support of His people. Paul's joy was not dependent upon himself or his circumstances, but on God and God's children. What a life-changing lesson for us to learn today! We can rejoice always because God will supply all our needs and He will send precious people to lift us up.

Paul was a grateful person. He not only felt gratitude in his heart, but he expressed it in words and actions to others. He spoke words of appreciation and he wrote words of thanks. He was genuinely thankful to God and others. His intention was both to teach the Philippians about the providence of God and how to graciously receive His blessings. It is important for contemporary Christians never to take God's gracious gifts for granted and to always respond gratefully to the kindness of others.

Grateful hearts are joyful hearts! Christians must always recognize the gifts from God and the generosity of others. "Thank you" is a powerful phrase. It expresses heartfelt appreciation from the receiver and conveys sincere encouragement to the giver. In order to experience joy, gratitude must be expressed. A verbal "thank you" can lift the spirits and a written "thank you" can minister to the soul. How long has it been since you have spoken words of appreciation to the Lord for all He has done for you? When was the last time you wrote a note of thanks to someone who was generous to you? It has been said that notes are "handwritten hugs that encircle what arms can't reach."

Take a few minutes to recall the goodness of God and the generosity of others.

On the next page, list the names of several people who have recently extended love to you and describe their acts of kindness.

103

Now write a prayer to the Lord, thanking Him for His sufficiency and the support of His children. I encourage you to also write a note of thanks to the people remembered above.

I am blessed to come from a family who outwardly expresses love and appreciation. Both of my parents are joyful, grateful people. "Thank you" was often expressed through words, hugs, and notes in our home. I grew up seeing my mother write notes of love and appreciation to her family and friends. She instilled in my sister and me the discipline of note writing. And today I receive great joy as I write notes to others. As I travel, my notes keep me connected with those I love but am apart from. I have developed a routine that reinforces my belief that written thank-you is not an option but a necessity. I discipline myself to write a note of appreciation to the church hostess where I have been in ministry before I can read a book or take a nap on the plane. My words of heartfelt gratitude remind me of the blessings of God and support of others. And I know the note encourages the receiver, who has ministered to me as unto the Lord.

My husband also was raised to be grateful. His parents are such affirming people. And his mother may hold the world record for number of notes written by one person in any given week. Her weekly family letters keep her children in touch. And her frequent notes to friends are treasures of love. It is such a blessing for me to help Mom Kelley communicate with others as I buy her notecards, stamps, and greeting cards. It is a privilege for me to mail her words of love which minister to many people.

Let me encourage you to become grateful like Paul the apostle. Express your gratitude both in verbal and written form. Don't contain your joy; share it with others. Just as you benefit from the gratitude expressed by others, they will be blessed by your words of appreciation. You may want to follow the advice of Barbara Johnson in her book *Splashes of Joy in the Cesspools of Life*. Decorate or find a "joy box" to hold notes of love and thanks. On those tough days, pull out a note or two and remember the love of others. You will rejoice! Now let's understand why Paul could always rejoice.

PAST PROVISION

In Philippians 4:10–23, Paul expressed his gratitude to the Philippians for their generous support, and he reminded them of the sufficiency of Christ. He was bubbling over with joy because of the goodness of God and his Christian friends. He explained why and when he was grateful. Paul could rejoice always because of past provision, present distress, and future glory. He began with a look back to remember how God provided.

Before we continue, read the focal passage in Philippians 4:10–23. As you read, underline reasons for rejoicing. Paul began his thank-yous by addressing the Christians in Philippi. He loved and appreciated them because they helped him. Their care for Paul had been a great help to him. This was not Paul's first time to say "thank you" to the Philippians. He had expressed gratitude previously in his letter. **Reread the following verses and summarize how Paul articulated his appreciation.**

Philippians 1:3–5—

Philippians 2:25–30—

Paul had attempted to convey to the Philippians his heartfelt gratitude for their help. He thanked them for their "fellowship in the gospel," recognizing their financial support of his ministry (Philippians 1:3–5). He thanked them for sending Epaphroditus to minister to his needs and sacrificially serve him (Philippians 2:25–30). His gratitude and joy are evident throughout this letter.

In Philippians 4:10–19, Paul tried to thank his generous friends more completely. His heart was so full of love and gratitude that he had difficulty expressing his feelings adequately. He appreciated their gifts even more knowing of their great sacrifice. The church in Philippi was financially poor, but they had given to Paul beyond their means. He was humbled by their sacrificial support.

Have you ever received generous gifts from an unselfish friend at a time of great financial need? If so, summarize how you felt when you were helped by another.

Because Paul's needs were so great, he was helped by many Christian friends. In several of his letters, he expressed his personal gratitude. Paul voiced his appreciation to various churches beautifully. In 2 Corinthians 8:1–5, he acknowledged their sacrificial giving.

"Moreover, brethren, we make known to you the grace of God bestowed on the churches of Macedonia: that in a great trial of affliction the abundance of their joy and their deep poverty abounded in the riches of their liberality. For I bear witness that according to their ability, yes, and beyond their ability, they were freely willing, imploring us with much urgency that we would receive the gift and the fellowship of the ministering to the saints. And not only as we had hoped, but they first gave themselves to the Lord, and then to us by the will of God."

Paul was grateful to the Christians who had helped him. He was greatly blessed by their generosity. **How did Paul describe their gifts in Philippians 4:18? Read that verse, then fill in the blanks below to describe their sacrificial support. Their gifts were like:**

a _____ - _____ aroma

an _____ sacrifice

well-pleasing to _____.

What a vivid description of the support of the saints! Our gifts to others are like a sweet-smelling aroma, an acceptable sacrifice, well pleasing to God.

Paul rejoiced in his past provision. Christians had helped and God had provided. He knew that all good and perfect gifts come from above (James 1:17). He reminded the Christians that God was the source of all in Philippians 4:19: "And my God shall supply all your need according to His riches in glory by Christ Jesus." Paul had learned to be content with what he had, knowing that God would always supply his needs (Philippians 4:11). He knew that God, the Provider, would also be his strength as he faced trials (Philippians 4:13). We, too, can rejoice because of past provision, and we can rejoice even in present distress.

PRESENT DISTRESS

Paul's joyful spirit was from the Lord, yet he rejoiced with his Christian friends. He was profoundly thankful for their support. Even as he suffered, he rejoiced, knowing of the love of the Father and the care of precious people. In Philippians 4:14–18, the apostle reminds his friends of his suffering for the sake of the gospel. Christians were aware of Paul's missionary zeal and his travels to share the gospel. On his first missionary journey, Paul along with Barnabas took the gospel to Galatia and Cyprus (Acts 13–14). On his second missionary journey, Paul with Silas and later Timothy spread the gospel to Macedonia, Achaia, and Greece (Acts 15:39–18:22). On his third missionary journey, Paul proclaimed the gospel in Asia and Greece (Acts 18:23–21:17). And on his fourth missionary journey, Paul preached the gospel in Caesarea, Crete, Malta, and Rome (Acts 27–28).

It was during his second missionary journey that Paul was first imprisoned for teaching the gospel. The Roman authorities and even the people found him guilty of heresy and stirring up trouble. During his imprisonment, he wrote this letter to the Christians in Philippi. Even though he suffered for his faith, he was joyful. In prison he experienced the joy of the Lord as he survived, and he shared the gospel even with the jailers. Throughout his letters, Paul honestly described his suffering because in his suffering God's faithfulness was apparent to all.

Read a few verses where Paul talked about his suffering. Summarize his feelings about his distress.

Romans 8:16–17—

Romans 8:18—

Philippians 1:29–30—

Philippians 3:8–9—

Paul understood that his suffering was a part of God's divine plan for his life. Because of his suffering, his faith was strengthened and his ministry was broadened. He concluded that his suffering was "with Him, that we may also be glorified together" (Romans 8:17). He knew that his own distress was "not worthy to be compared with the glory which shall be revealed in us" (Romans 8:18). Paul wanted to "suffer for His sake" (Philippians 1:29). His love for the Lord was so deep that he willingly suffered to share the truth of the gospel. And he actually felt blessed to suffer for his Lord—"I also count all things loss for the excellence of the knowledge of Christ Jesus my Lord, for whom I have suffered the loss of all things" (Philippians 3:8). He rejoiced in his sufferings, and we Christians today should rejoice in the Lord even when we experience our own personal trials and minor inconveniences.

Christians in America today don't really know what it means to suffer for the gospel. Most of us are able to worship the Lord freely and share the gospel openly. But we must be willing to stand up for our faith even if it means persecution or penalty. Many Christians throughout history and throughout the world today have suffered for their faith like Paul, and they, too, have rejoiced in the Lord.

In the third century, there lived a Christian noblewoman in Carthage (modern Tunis) named Perpetua who suffered for her faith. While this mother of an infant child was taking classes to prepare for her baptism, she was arrested. Her pagan father visited her in prison and begged her to deny her faith. She refused, and she was doomed to die. Her strong stance is a powerful lesson for us today. She asked her father, "Could this vase be called by any other name than what it is?" When he replied negatively, she responded: "Well neither can I be called anything other than what I am, a Christian." Her father approached her again, but she continued to defend her faith. Along with other Christians, Perpetua was attacked by wild animals in an arena as a public spectacle, then killed with a sword. The testimony of her faith was so significant that Augustine, the great theologian of the Middle Ages, preached four sermons about her death (*131 Christians Everyone Should Know*, 362–363).

I recently heard the testimony of a precious seminary student from the Ukraine who suffered for her faith under Communist rule. As a fourth grader from a Christian family, she learned that the government would deny education to any child who attended church. She was faced with a difficult choice—stand firm in her faith and lose her opportunity for education, or deny her faith and remain in school. Though the decision was difficult and had life-changing implications, she went to church on Sunday with her family. Her teacher was outside the church taking names of school children who defied the authorities. God blessed Tetyana's faithfulness. She was allowed to finish high school in her own country, and now she is completing college in America. God honored her because she rejoiced in Him.

Paul wrote to the Philippians about his suffering and his imprisonment. He was actually put in jail several times during his ministry (Acts 16:16–40; 23:23–26:32; 27–28). Each sentence gave him opportunities to witness to unsaved soldiers and write letters to Christian friends. He concluded in

Philippians 1:12–14 that "the things which happened to me have actually turned out for the furtherance of the gospel, so that it has become evident to the whole palace guard, and to all the rest, that my chains are in Christ; and most of the brethren in the Lord, having become confident by my chains, are much more bold to speak the word without fear."

Have you ever suffered for the gospel or even faced personal trials because of your faith? If so, what did you learn through that experience? How has your life been affected by suffering?

Like Paul and the apostle Peter, you can grow in Christ when you face trials—"You have been grieved by various trials, that the genuineness of your faith, being much more precious than gold that perishes, though it is tested by fire, may be found to praise, honor, and glory at the revelation of Jesus Christ" (1 Peter 1:6–7). Paul rejoiced in his past provision, in his present distress, and in his future glory.

FUTURE GLORY

In this passage, Paul remembered God's provision of the past, he rejoiced in God's protection in the present, and he rested in God's promise for the future. He no longer spoke in the past tense, but in the future tense. And he spoke with great confidence, "my God *shall* supply all your need according to His riches in glory by Christ Jesus" (Philippians 4:19). He reminded them that God *would receive* glory forever and ever (Philippians 4:20). Paul thanked the Philippians for their support. But he recognized that while they met *one* of his needs, God would supply *all* his needs. That promise gave Paul hope for the future.

Dependence on God for all personal needs was a common theme of Paul's letters to the New Testament churches. In 2 Corinthians, he wrote to the Christians about generous giving. He taught them that Christ loves a cheerful giver (2 Corinthians 9:7). He then explained why Christians can give cheerfully and generously even when they have little. **Read 2 Corinthians 9:10–15. Now answer these questions from a biblical viewpoint.**

Who supplies all resources?

Why does He increase resources?

Who benefits from giving?

Who is glorified?

God is ultimately the source of all that we have. He gives to us abundantly to supply all our needs, not all our greeds. He increases our resources so that we can give to others. Both the giver and receiver benefit from the gift. Giving is always a double blessing, and the glory goes to God. As Paul concluded in 2 Corinthians 9:15: "Thanks be to God for His indescribable gift!"

Paul knew that God would always protect him and provide for him. He wanted to glorify God and experience the glory of God. **What is "the glory of God?"**

We often sing about the glory of God, but we must also understand it. The glory of God is certainly His divine power and majesty revealed to us. While His children can know the glory of God now, one day all people will see the glory of God. When He returns again, we will see him in all of His glory (1 John 3:2–3), and we shall be transformed into His glory (Philippians 3:20–21). There will be great rejoicing when we enter the brightness of heaven, for the glory of God illuminates it (Revelation 21:23). His glory in the present and in the future gave Paul tremendous joy. Christians today should be joyful as we experience God's glory in our hearts and anticipate God's glory in heaven.

Paul's final greeting was typical of New Testament letters. In Philippians 4:21–22, he sent fond greetings to believers ("saints") in Philippi. His previous comments had been addressed to believers generally (Philippians 1:1, 3, 12; 2:4; 3:1, 17; 4:1, 21, 23). Now Paul wants every individual believer to heed his words ("every saint"). While Paul extended a personal greeting, he asked every saint to greet another saint. He sought to involve all Christians in spreading the gospel. He taught by the multiplication principle—if one person tells one person, then many people will know. Many of Paul's letters were considered circular letters to be passed from one church to another. His final greeting to the Philippians was a circular farewell.

In addition, his greeting was not just from himself but from Christians who were with him. He extended special greetings from those "of Caesar's household" (Philippians 4:22). That term applied to all those in Roman civil service, both slaves and free. Paul had led many Romans to faith in Christ; some may have even been from Philippi. His greetings were both general (to all saints, from all saints) and specific (to an individual believer, from Paul).

There is a parallel among Christians today. The pastor may share a message to all the congregation, though it speaks directly to one person. One person will ask another to say hello to a mutual friend. The greeting is transmitted through an individual. In the worship service, a minister welcomes the people and encourages each member to greet another. And the gospel is spread from one Christian to one unbeliever. God's plan of redemption and fellowship is often fulfilled through His children one by one.

In the last verse, Paul gave his benediction: "The grace of our Lord Jesus Christ be with you all. Amen" (Philippians 4:23). Paul often closed his letters with a prayer for God's grace to abound in his Christian friends (see 1 Corinthians 16:23; 2 Corinthians 13:14; Galatians 6:18; Ephesians 6:24; Colossians 4:18; 1 Thessalonians 5:28; 2 Thessalonians 3:18; 1 Timothy 6:21; 2 Timothy 4:22; Titus 3:15; Philemon 25). He had received the precious grace of God, and he wanted all his Christian friends to experience God's grace as well.

The joy of the Lord was evident in Paul as he closed his letter to the Philippians. He could rejoice always because of his past provision, his present distress, and his future glory. Can you rejoice always? It is my prayer that you will rejoice in the Lord now and forever more.

CONCLUSION

As I have been writing and teaching this Bible study, a friend gave me a journal. The cover is beautiful—a tea set with a floral background in my favorite colors of rose, blue, and yellow. It bears the words: "Joy grows when life is shared with family and friends." I have certainly found that to be true in my life. My joy grows as I build my relationship with my Heavenly Father as well as strengthen relationships with those I love. My growing faith and commitment to Him intensifies my joy. During this study of the Book of Philippians, I have learned so much about God Himself, His gift of salvation, and His gracious provision. I have deepened my love for His Word. And I pray that you, too, have grown in your love for the Lord and you can enthusiastically rejoice in Him.

Reflecting back on the Book of Philippians, I realize how many profound teachings are included in this short letter. Paul thoroughly discussed two significant biblical doctrines—Christology and justification by faith. It is so important to understand who Jesus Christ is and how to be saved. Paul also considered God—His nature, His plan, and His provisions. He spoke directly to us about life, suffering, and circumstances. Paul challenged us to joyful, godly living. And he affirmed God's promise of heaven. Christians can benefit immensely from a study of the New Testament epistle.

Before you conclude this study, take a few minutes to make some personal commitments. List below some personal goals for growing in your ability to live joyfully.

Joyful Living

1. I will

2. I will

3. I will

4. I will

5. I will

Now spend some time in prayer. Ask God to help you to accomplish your goals for joyful living. Consider sharing your commitments with a friend, possibly someone in your Bible study group.

God will empower you as you seek Him, and Christian friends will encourage you as well as hold you accountable. Remember what Paul said in Philippians 1:3–6:

"I thank my God upon every remembrance of you, always in every prayer of mine making request for you all with joy, for your fellowship in the gospel from the first day until now, being confident of this very thing, that He who has begun a good work in you will complete it until the day of Jesus Christ."

Christians can have the confidence of Paul that joy will always come in the morning. God who is the giver of joy will graciously pour out joy upon us no matter what our circumstances. We can cling to that hope and promise. We can find true joy. We can live a godly life.

This section includes some teaching suggestions for the small group leader. It also provides a format for the discussion time and a typical schedule for a one-hour session. This particular group approach has been tried successfully with a focus group. However, let the Holy Spirit lead your group discussion and make any appropriate changes. These are simply teaching helps.

LESSON ONE: REJOICE IN THE LORD

Prayer Time (5 minutes)
Spend the first few minutes of this session sharing praises. Ask the ladies to focus only upon their reasons for rejoicing. Then ask a volunteer to lead a prayer of praise.

Review (5 minutes)
Discuss the format of this study and details about the group meetings. Encourage each member to complete her own study before discussing it with the group. Also challenge them to make a commitment to complete the study.

Introduction (5 minutes)
Begin this study with a discussion about *joy*. What is joy and why is joy important to a Christian? Read the definitions of joy in the book and explain that one theme of the Book of Philippians is joy. Ask the ladies to "consider it all joy" as they study this inspiring book of the Bible.

Group Discussion (40 minutes)
1. Have one group member read Galatians 5:22–23. Then discuss joy as a fruit of the Spirit. Briefly review the three sections in the book—*who, how,* and *why* rejoice.

2. Read the focal passage—Philippians 1:1–11. Discuss the author of the book and the audience. Refer to the specific questions in this lesson.

3. Ask the group to consider how Paul rejoiced. Refer to Philippians 1:3–8 for a description. Then ask them how they rejoice in the Lord.

4. Briefly discuss *why* Christians should rejoice. Also ask, "Why is prayer a part of rejoicing?"

5. Suggest that each person make a commitment to rejoice in the Lord in all things. Discuss how they will rejoice. Encourage practical suggestions of how they will be joyful.

Closing (5 minutes)
Ask group members to spend a few minutes in silent prayer making commitments to the Lord and to complete this study. As leader, voice a closing prayer aloud. Pray for the group members during the week and try to let them know you are praying.

LESSON TWO: REJOICE IN THE GOSPEL

Prayer Time (5 minutes)
Open with prayer, rejoicing in God's blessings and thanking Him for the gift of the gospel. Ask Him to empower all believers to spread the Good News.

Review (5 minutes)
Review Lesson One by asking the following questions:
1. Who wrote Philippians?
2. To whom was it written?
3. Why was it written?
Then briefly summarize the book's theme of joy. Ask the ladies to share how their joyful spirits encouraged others this past week.

Introduction (5 minutes)
Briefly discuss the meaning of the word "gospel." Ask group members to share their brief one-sentence definitions. Then have someone read the definitions noted in this lesson. Consider the question: "Why is the gospel a reason for rejoicing?"

Group Discussion (40 minutes)
1. Read Philippians 1:12–18 aloud from several translations. Ask: "What does Paul tell his Christian friends in Philippi about the gospel?"

2. Ask class members who are willing to briefly share their conversion experiences. Challenge all to accept the gospel personally.

3. Seek a volunteer to read Romans 2:1–10. Then answer these questions: How did Paul defend the gospel? How do you defend the gospel? Why does the gospel need defending?

4. Reread Philippians 1:15–18 and discuss how Paul preached the gospel.

Also read 2 Timothy 1:8–12. Explain how Christians can boldly preach the gospel.

5. Discuss how to overcome the fear of sharing the gospel. Read Paul's confession and commitment in 1 Corinthians 2:1–5. Talk about how to overcome the fear of sharing the gospel.

Closing (5 minutes)

In closing, ask members to pray silently for a lost friend or family member. Make a commitment to share your faith with them and continue praying for their salvation. Ask a volunteer to close the session in prayer rejoicing in the gospel.

LESSON THREE: REJOICE IN LIFE

Prayer Time (5 minutes)

Ask group members to pair up for prayer. Allow time for each person to share a personal life challenge. Then suggest that they pray for each other and conclude by praising God for His guidance and strength.

Review (5 minutes)

Briefly review last week's lesson about the gospel. Focus on why Paul specifically and Christians generally should believe that the gospel is reason for rejoicing.

Introduction (5 minutes)

Take a few minutes to talk about life—its joys and sorrows. Then challenge the group to always rejoice whether life is good or bad, knowing that God is in control.

Group Discussion (40 minutes)

1. Ask someone to read Philippians 1:19–26, then discuss Paul's feelings about his Christian friends and about his life's circumstances.

2. Solicit several statements from the group about life (i.e. "Life is good," "Life is tough," "Life is changing," etc.). Read John 10:10, then discuss its meaning.

3. Discuss why Christians can rejoice in death. Have group members read aloud Scriptures about heaven—Genesis 1:8, Psalm 19:1, and Hebrews 4:14. Spend a few minutes talking about heaven, then read Revelation 21:1–7.

4. Make a list on the board of pros and cons about living and dying. Why would it be better to live? List reasons. Why would it be better to die? List reasons.

5. Conclude your group discussion with confidence—God's will is best! Ask someone to reread Philippians 1:19–26.

Closing (5 minutes)
Close with conversational prayer, sharing personal prayer requests and concluding with confidence in God's concern and control.

LESSON FOUR: REJOICE IN SUFFERING

Prayer Time (5 minutes)
Spend a few minutes in prayer for the suffering people of the world. Ask three group members to pray aloud—one for the suffering of your city, one for the suffering of the nation, and another for the suffering of the world.

Review (5 minutes)
Briefly review what Paul felt about life and death in Philippians 1:19–26. Summarize your own conclusions and challenge the group to always rejoice in God's best whether it is life or death.

Introduction (5 minutes)
Introduce the topic of suffering by briefly discussing the suffering in the Bible, the suffering of the world, and suffering of every Christian. Inform the ladies that this lesson will remind us why Christians can rejoice even in suffering. Though suffering is painful, God can give joy.

Group Discussion (40 minutes)
1. Ask the group members if they have ever suffered adversity and what they learned through it. Now read Paul's testimony in Philippians 1:27–2:4.

2. Remind the group that Christians often suffer for the sake of Christ. Ask someone to summarize the suffering of Stephen, then read Acts 7:54–60.

3. Discuss the reality of personal suffering and why a Christian should rejoice in suffering. Read James 1:2–8 for a biblical basis.

4. Consider the suffering of others and how to support them. Ask the group members how they express concern, comfort, and care to those who suffer.

5. Read Romans 12:9–16 to see how Paul ministered to those who were suffering and how we should care for others as well.

Closing (5 minutes)
As a group, decide on one instance of suffering in your church or community that you want to pray about. Discuss a specific way your group can minister to that person, then pray for God to help your group reach out to those who are suffering and rejoice in your own suffering.

LESSON FIVE: REJOICE IN JESUS

Prayer Time (5 minutes)

In the opening prayer time, use the acrostic JOY (Jesus—Others—You) to guide the sentence prayers. First, express praise to *Jesus* for who He is and what He has done. Then lift up petitions on the behalf of *others* (prayer concerns about others). Finally, voice requests for *yourself.* Remember that God hears and answers prayer.

Review (5 minutes)

Briefly review the last lesson about suffering. Remind the group members how to rejoice in suffering for His sake, your sake, and their sakes. Christians should rejoice in their own suffering and minister to those who are suffering.

Introduction (5 minutes)

Inform the group that this lesson focuses on the nature of Jesus. Briefly discuss who He is (Christology) and why Christians can rejoice in Christ. Challenge the members to understand Jesus Christ to the best of their human ability.

Group Discussion (40 minutes)

1. Read the focal passage—Philippians 2:5–18. Ask the group members how God describes His Son Jesus Christ in this Scripture and other passages.

2. Discuss the divinity of Jesus—He is God. Read another key Christological passage from Colossians 1:5–18. How is Christ described as God?

3. Discuss the humanity of Jesus—He was Man. Read John 1:14–18. How is Christ described as Man?

4. Discuss the Trinity—God the Father, Jesus the Son, and the Holy Spirit. Read Hebrews 1:1–4. Ask the ladies if they are beginning to understand the full nature of Jesus Christ.

5. Conclude your discussion by celebrating Christ as Savior. You may want to lead the group in singing a song about Jesus, such as "Since Jesus Came Into My Heart," or "I've Got the Joy, Joy, Joy."

Closing (5 minutes)

Ask the ladies to write a love letter to the Lord, a prayer of thankfulness to Jesus. They can leave the room quietly as they finish their prayertime.

LESSON SIX: REJOICE WITH OTHERS

Prayer Time (5 minutes)
Give out index cards to group members and ask each one to record a prayer concern for another person. Allow time for silent prayer for that petition, then close the prayer time yourself.

Review (5 minutes)
Spend a few minutes discussing who Jesus is (God, man, Savior). Then ask ladies to share ways that Jesus has made Himself known to them personally this past week.

Introduction (5 minutes)
Remind the ladies that Paul was "being poured out as a drink offering on the sacrifice and service of faith" (Philippians 2:17). Discuss how the suffering of some Christians can be a blessing to others. In this lesson we will examine how to encourage others, support others, and esteem others.

Group Discussion (40 minutes)
1. Ask a group member to read Philippians 2:19–30, then answer these questions: Who did Paul commend? How did he praise them? Why did he praise them?

2. Read aloud Ephesians 4:25–32. Make a list of key words or phrases of instruction. Discuss why these instructions are necessary for Christians to encourage others.

3. Who was Epaphroditus? (Refer to Philippians 2:25–30 for this answer.) Discuss how he supported Paul and other Christians. Ask how Christians today can support each other.

4. Discuss the word *esteem*, then call on someone to read 1 Thessalonians 5:12–19. How can you esteem others?

5. Reread 1 Thessalonians 5:16–18, then complete these phrases: rejoice _____, _____ without ceasing, and in _____ give thanks. (See the Scripture or the lesson for answers.) Have everyone repeat the phrases aloud.

Closing (5 minutes)
Ask the group members to exchange their prayer cards with each other. Conclude with sentence prayers for these specific concerns. Rejoice in the privilege of praying for others.

LESSON SEVEN: REJOICE IN CIRCUMSTANCES

Prayer Time (5 minutes)
During the opening prayer time, ask the ladies to honestly evaluate what they have learned about joy and how they are rejoicing. Spend time in personal prayer renewing the initial commitment to God and this Bible study.

Review (5 minutes)
Take a few minutes to remind the group of last week's study about rejoicing with others. Ask them how they have encouraged others, supported others, and esteemed others this past week.

Introduction (5 minutes)
Try to describe how Paul could rejoice in his circumstances, not his credentials. Ask the group members to consider why Paul could rejoice even in his difficult circumstances and why Christians today can rejoice. Remind them of God's promise to give joy even in the toughest times.

Group Discussion (40 minutes)
1. Ask someone to read Philippians 3:1–11—this lesson's focal passage. Briefly discuss Paul's personal credentials in verses 5 and 6. What are the personal credentials of members in the group? Remember that joy is available to the Christian because of Christ, not credentials.

2. Discuss Paul's warning in Philippians 3:2–3 about the "false circumcision." How can we rejoice when we face adversaries and false teachers? Also read Galatians 1:6–10 and discuss how Christians can help new believers resist untrue doctrine.

3. Review Paul's "losses" and "gains" as described in Philippians 3:7–11, then complete the statements in the book that declare how Christians can rejoice when facing difficult circumstances.

4. Consider the consequences of bad choices. Ask the group members who are willing to share what God taught them through their bad choices. Rejoice in God's forgiveness of His fallen children (1 John 1:9).

5. Read again Philippians 3:1–11. Ask the ladies to suggest guidelines for good judgment. Challenge them to follow those godly guidelines and rejoice in all their circumstances.

Closing (5 minutes)
Ask the group members to repeat aloud Philippians 3:10, then pray it as a prayer— "Lord, Help me know You, the power of Your resurrection, and the fellowship of Your suffering."

LESSON EIGHT: REJOICE IN GOD'S PLAN

Prayer Time (5 minutes)

Give every person an index card and ask each lady to pray honestly about anything in her past that has hurt her relationship to Christ. Write it on the card and consider it during the lesson. Pray for God to bring forgiveness to all His children.

Review (5 minutes)

Help the group members remember Paul's biblical guidelines in last week's lesson. Christians should rejoice in circumstances—when facing the false circumcision, enduring difficult circumstances, and making bad choices.

Introduction (5 minutes)

Explain that this lesson considers God's plan and how to rejoice in it. Read Jeremiah 29:11–13 and discuss what the Bible teaches about God's plan for every believer.

Group Discussion (40 minutes)

1. Read the very familiar passage in Philippians 3:12–16. If possible, have someone read it in *The Message* paraphrase for modern-day insights. Ask the group if they are seeking to know and follow God's plan. How?

2. Ask: "Why is it important for Christians to forget the past?" Read the following Scriptures, then discuss what the Bible teaches about forgiveness—Psalm 103:12, Isaiah 1:18, Micah 7:19, Romans 3:25, and Hebrews 10:17.

3. Next, consider Paul's second instruction in this passage. He said, "reach ahead." Read Philippians 3:12–14 and discuss the results of "pressing on," "reaching forward," and "pressing toward."

4. Paul also instructed Christians to "press upward." Read Hebrews 12:1–2 and discuss why it is important to press upward. Also answer these questions: What should we lay aside? How should we run? Where should we look? What is set before us?

5. Remember that Christians are encouraged by other faithful Christians. Who is the "great cloud of witnesses" in Hebrews 12:1? How do they help us rejoice in God's plan?

Closing (5 minutes)

As you close this session, ask each person to look back at her index card, which records a past transgression that needs to be forgiven by God. Pray a prayer of forgiveness, then tear up the card as a reminder of God's complete forgiveness and His perfect plan for your life.

LESSON NINE: REJOICE IN THE PROMISE OF HEAVEN

Prayer Time (5 minutes)
Encourage the group members to meditate on the future as you begin your prayer time. Allow time for them to seek God about their future here on earth and in heaven. Remember to praise God even as you face the uncertainties of the future.

Review (5 minutes)
Review God's plan as discussed by Paul in Philippians 3:12–16. Briefly summarize why people should "forget the past," "reach ahead," and "press upward."

Introduction (5 minutes)
Spend a few minutes asking members to discuss anything they have ever heard or believed about heaven. Read John 14:1–3 and remind the group that Christians can rejoice in the promise of heaven.

Group Discussion (40 minutes)
1. Ask each group member to silently read Philippians 3:17–21. Answer these questions: Who are the "enemies of the cross" and who would be "friends of the cross?"

2. Discuss citizenship and dual citizenship. Why is dual citizenship important to Christians? Then explain the place called heaven.

3. Select a person to read 2 Peter 3:10–13. What does Peter say about heaven and the presence of God? Write on the board some possible heavenly activities.

4. Take a few minutes for the ladies to list things about their bodies they do not like. Then remind them of their perfect bodies in heaven. Read Philippians 3:21 as well as Psalm 139:14–17 for God's opinion of our bodies.

5. In closing, read John 3:5–7 as a reminder that only those who are saved will go to heaven. Ask the group to discuss some different views about how people will go to heaven (good works, going to church, birthright, etc.). Remember God's requirement for entry into heaven.

Closing (5 minutes)
During the closing prayer time, pray for those who are not saved and will not spend eternity in heaven. Ask the ladies to pray sentence prayers for their salvation. Then close in confidence that God can save.

LESSON TEN: REJOICE IN PRAYER

Prayer Time (5 minutes)
Spend some time sharing some praises of how God is working in the lives of people. Ask three ladies to pray aloud specifically in *praise* to God, with *petitions* for others, and for *power* from God.

Review (5 minutes)
Briefly summarize several biblical teachings about heaven—the place, His presence, and our perfection. Ask the ladies what God has been teaching them about heaven, His eternal home.

Introduction (5 minutes)
Begin this lesson with a discussion about prayer. Ask a volunteer to read Philippians 4:4–7, then share perspectives on prayer. Share the names of real prayer warriors and thank God for them.

Group Discussion (40 minutes)
1. Read today's focal passage in Philippians 4:1–7. What two-fold recommendation did Paul make to unite the women and bring harmony to the church? Challenge the ladies to pray about disharmony in their churches.

2. Ask the group members to honestly explain whether or not prayer is a priority in their lives. Seek suggestions of some helpful prayer resources.

3. Read Philippians 4:6 again to discover what God teaches about prayer. Then discuss these prayer words: supplication, request, and petition.

4. Ask: "What did Jesus teach His disciples about the promise of prayer?" Have someone read John 14:13–14, and discuss the answer. How has God fulfilled His promise about prayer in your life?

5. On the board write "yes," "no," and "wait" at the top of three columns. Guide the class in identifying prayers that could be answered by God with yes, no, or wait. List them in the appropriate column. Read Philippians 4:7 in conclusion.

Closing (5 minutes)
Ask the group to pray in triads (3 ladies in a group). Each one should pray specifically, including a praise, a petition, and for power much like the opening prayer, but this time in small groups.

LESSON ELEVEN: REJOICE IN GODLY VIRTUES

Prayer Time (5 minutes)
During this opening prayer time, mention specific prayer concerns within your church. Pray for the pastor and staff, the sick and grieving, and the ministries of the church.

Review (5 minutes)
As you begin, review last week's study on prayer. Briefly discuss the purpose and priority of prayer. Then read Philippians 4:1–7.

Introduction (5 minutes)
Take a few minutes to recall the ungodliness of the world (war, violence, crime, etc.). Now discuss the importance of godliness among Christians. Paul challenged Christians to think godly thoughts and do godly deeds.

Group Discussion (40 minutes)
1. Ask group members to read Philippians 4:8–9 in all the translations represented in the room. What godly virtues should Christians meditate on? List them on the board.

2. Ask someone to read Psalm 19:7–9. Discuss similar virtues of God's Word and godly lives.

3. Write Paul's formula for godly living on the board. List these steps from Philippians 4:9—*learn, receive, hear, see,* and *do.* Discuss this as a process of sanctification.

4. Recall some of the godly deeds of Jesus. Ask volunteers to read the following accounts: Matthew 8:14–15; Mark 5:33–42; Luke 13:10–14; and John 2:1–11. Describe how Jesus led a godly life.

5. Write the names of these five women of the Bible on the board—Rahab, Esther, Martha, Dorcas, and Lydia. Ask volunteers to read the following Scriptures, then match each woman with her godly deed—Joshua 2:1–24; Esther 8:1–17; John 12:1–2; Acts 9:36–42; and Acts 16:11–15.

Closing (5 minutes)
In this closing prayer, ask the ladies to pray specifically for the lady on her right—"May the God of peace be with you" (Philippians 4:9). Go around the room until everyone has been prayed for and everyone has prayed. Then close with "Amen."

LESSON TWELVE: REJOICE ALWAYS

Prayer Time (5 minutes)

Cut from a current newspaper some specific prayer concerns in your community, the country, and the world. Circulate the articles, asking ladies to pray specifically for these needs.

Review (5 minutes)

Briefly summarize the last lesson about godly virtues. Read Philippians 4:8 and ask the ladies how they rejoiced in godly virtues this past week.

Introduction (5 minutes)

Begin today's study with a reminder that Christians should rejoice at all times. Read several verses in Philippians that teach us to rejoice—Philippians 1:4, 1:18, 1:25–26, 2:2, 2:17–18, 3:1, and 4:10.

Group Discussion (40 minutes)

1. Ask the ladies to share how they have experienced the goodness of God and the generosity of others. Encourage them to be gracious to others.

2. Have a volunteer read the focal passage in Philippians 4:10–23. Guide the group in identifying all words and phrases that describe how Paul expressed gratitude to the Philippian Christians. Which verse or phrase expresses your gratitude for the generosity of others? Then read Philippians 4:18.

3. Recall how Paul rejoiced even in his suffering. Ask group members to again read Philippians 1:29–30 and 3:8–9. How can we rejoice in present distress?

4. Focus attention on the "glory of God" in Philippians 4:20. Discuss how Christians can rejoice in the future. Read Paul's closing in Philippians 4:21–23.

5. Ask each lady to share a special verse from the Book of Philippians. How has God used that verse to teach her to have true joy?

Closing (5 minutes)

Ask each member of the group to write a commitment to rejoice in the back of her Bible study book. Then ask prayer partners to pray for each other to know the joy of the Lord.

BIBLIOGRAPHY

Barclay, William. *The Letters to the Philippians, Colossians, and Thessalonians* (Revised Edition) (Philadephia: The Westminister Press, 1975).

Barnes, Emilie. *A Different Kind Of Miracle* (Eugene, OR: Harvest House Publishers, 2002).

Butler, Trent C. *Holman Bible Dictionary* (Nashville: Holman Bible Publishers, 1991).

Craddock, Fred. *Intrepretation: A Bible Commentary for Teaching and Preaching Philippians* (Atlanta: John Knox Press, 1985).

Dean, Jennifer Kennedy. *Live a Praying Life* (Birmingham: New Hope Publishers, 2003).

Dunnam, Maxie D. *The Communicator's Commentary: Galatians, Ephesians, Philippians, Colossians, Philemon* (Waco: Word Books, 1982).

Fromer, Margaret and Paul. *A Woman's Workshop on Philippians* (Grand Rapids: Zondervan Publishing House, 1982).

Galli, Mark and Ted Olsen (eds.). *131 Christians Everyone Should Know* (Nashville: Broadman & Holman Publishers, 2000).

Johnson, Barbara. *Splashes of Joy in the Cesspools of Life* (Dallas: Word Publishing Group, 1992).

Kelley, Rhonda H. *Don't Miss the Blessing Study Guide* (Gretna, LA: Pelican Publishing Company, 1990).

Kelley, Rhonda H. *Life Lessons from Women in the Bible* (Nashville: LifeWay Press, 1998).

Leavell, JoAnn Paris. *Don't Miss the Blessing* (Gretna, LA: Pelican Publishing Company, 1990).

Lotz, Anne Graham. *The Vision of His Glory: Finding Hope Through the Revelation of Jesus Christ* (Dallas: Word Publishing, 1996).

Merriam-Webster's Collegiate Dictionary (Springfield, MA: Merriam-Webster, 1997).

Schreiner, Thomas R. *Intrepreting the Pauline Epistles* (Grand Rapids: Baker Book House, 1990).

Shepherd, David R.(ed.). *Shepherd's Notes Philippians/Colossians/Philemon* (Nashville: Broadman & Holman Publishers, 1997).

Tada, Joni Eareckson. *Heaven: Your Real Home* (Nashville: LifeWay Press, 1996).

Taylor, Preston. *Philippians: Joy in Jesus* (Orlando: Daniels Publishers, Inc., 1976).

The Woman's Study Bible (Nashville: Thomas Nelson Publishers, 1995).

Wiersbe, Warren W. *Be Joyful: Even When Things Go Wrong You Can Have Joy* (Wheaton, IL: Victor Books, 1988).

APPENDIX A

There are many key passages in the Book of Philippians. Here are a few verses that should bring you joy.

Philippians 1:9— "And this I pray, that your love may abound still more and more in knowledge and all discernment."

Philippians 1:21— "For to me, to live is Christ, and to die is gain."

Philippians 2:3— "Let nothing be done through selfish ambition or conceit, but in lowliness of mind let each esteem others better than himself."

Philippians 3:13–14— "Brethren, I do not count myself to have apprehended; but one thing I do, forgetting those things which are behind and reaching forward to those things which are ahead, I press toward the goal for the prize of the upward call of God in Christ Jesus."

Philippians 4:6— "Be anxious for nothing, but in everything by prayer and supplication, with thanksgiving, let your requests be made known to God."

Philippians 4:8— "Finally, brethren, whatever things are true, whatever things are noble, whatever things are just, whatever things are pure, whatever things are lovely, whatever things are of good report, if there is any virtue and if there is anything praiseworthy—meditate on these things."

Philippians 4:13— "I can do all things through Christ who strengthens me."

Philippians 4:19— "And my God shall supply all your need according to His riches in glory by Christ Jesus."

APPENDIX B

SONGS OF JOY

There are so many songs about joy.
Here are just a few:

"Break Forth Into Joy"

"Rejoice in the Lord Always"

"Break Into Songs of Joy"

"Rejoice Ye Pure in Heart"

"Come Let us Sing for Joy to the Lord"

"Ring the Bells of Heaven"

"Come, We That Love the Lord"

"Serve the Lord with Gladness"

"Good Christian Men, Rejoice"

"Since Jesus Came Into My Heart"

"He Has Made Me Glad"

"Sing and Rejoice"

"How Great Our Joy"

"Sing a Joyful Song"

"I Come With Joy to Meet My Lord"

"Sunshine in My Soul"

"I Will Celebrate"

"The Celebration Song"

"I Will Rejoice"

"The Joy of the Lord is My Strength"

"In the Presence of the Lord"

"There is Joy in the Lord"

"I've Got Peace Like a River"

"Therefore the Redeemed"

"I've Got the Joy, Joy, Joy"

"There's A Glad New Song"

"Jerusalem, My Happy Home"

"This is the Day"

"Let the Earth Rejoice"

"This Joy That I Have"

"Let the Heavens Rejoice"

"Trading My Sorrows"

"Lord, Make Our Homes"

"We Bring the Sacrifice of Praise"

"Near to the Heart of God"

"We have Heard the Joyful Sound"

"Of All the Spirit's Gifts to Me"

"We're Marching to Zion"

Also in the Woman's Guide series by
Rhonda H. Kelley

These 12-week Bible studies guide women to deeper levels of spiritual health and wholeness. All contain facilitator's guides.

1-56309-435-5
A WOMAN'S GUIDE TO
PERSONAL DISCIPLINE
*A Biblical Study of Self-Control
and Perseverance*

1-56309-434-7
A WOMAN'S GUIDE TO
SERVANT LEADERSHIP
*A Biblical Study for Becoming
a Christlike Leader*

1-56309-433-9
A WOMAN'S GUIDE TO
TRUE CONTENTMENT
*A Biblical Study for Achieving
Satisfaction in Life*

1-56309-432-0
A WOMAN'S GUIDE TO
PERSONAL HOLINESS
*A Biblical Study for Developing
a Holy Lifestyle*

1-56309-252-2
A WOMAN'S GUIDE TO
SPIRITUAL WELLNESS
A Personal Study of Colossians

Available in Christian bookstores everywhere.

NEW HOPE
PUBLISHERS